The Best Things Anybody Ever Said About Sports, Management, & Marketing

Louis E. Boone
David L. Kurtz

Australia · Canada · Mexico · Singapore · Spain · United Kingdom · United States

The Best Things Anybody Ever Said About Sports, Management, and Marketing

Louis E. Boone and David L. Kurtz

VP/Editorial Director:
Jack W. Calhoun

VP/Editor-in-Chief:
Dave Shaut

Sr. Publisher:
Melissa Acuña

Acquisitions Editor:
Neil Marquardt

Sr. Developmental Editor:
Susan Smart

Marketing Manager:
Nicole Moore

Production Editor:
Starratt Alexander

Manager of Technology, Editorial:
Vicky True

Technology Project Editor:
Pam Wallace

Web Coordinator:
Karen L. Schaffer

Sr. First Print Buyer:
Diane Lohman

Production House:
OffCenter Concept House

Art Director:
Stacy Shirley

Internal Designer:
OffCenter Concept House

Cover Designer:
Liz Harasymczuk Design

Cover Images:
© Getty Images and © Corbis

Printer:
Malloy Lithographing, Inc.
Ann Arbor, Michigan

Printed in the United States of America
1 2 3 4 5 08 07 06 05

ISBN: 0-324-32283-6

Library of Congress Control Number:
2004117357

For more information about our products, contact us at:
Thomson Learning Academic Resource Center
1-800-423-0563

Thomson Higher Education
5191 Natorp Boulevard
Mason, OH 45040
USA

Asia (including India)
Thomson Learning
5 Shenton Way
#01-01 UIC Building
Singapore 068808

Australia/New Zealand
Thomson Learning Australia
102 Dodds Street
Southbank, Victoria 3006
Australia

Canada
Thomson Nelson
1120 Birchmount Road
Toronto, Ontario
M1K 5G4
Canada

Latin America
Thomson Learning
Seneca, 53
Colonia Polanco
11560 Mexico
D.F.Mexico

UK/Europe/Middle East/Africa
Thomson Learning
High Holborn House
50/51 Bedford Row
London WC1R 4LR
United Kingdom

Spain (including Portugal)
Thomson Paraninfo
Calle Magallanes, 25
28015 Madrid, Spain

CONTENTS

Other Books by LOUIS E. BOONE and DAVID L. KURTZ

CEO: Who Gets to the Top in America?
(with C. Patrick Fleenor)

Contemporary Business

Contemporary Marketing

Planning Your Financial Future

Quotable Business

The Impact of Terrorism

To Louis W. Boone and C. Reed Kurtz,
whose reminiscences of long-ago sports greats are
among our earliest and fondest memories.

PREFACE

Sports have been an inherent part of society almost as long as men and women have walked the face of the planet. Rudolph Brasch, in his book *How Did Sports Begin?* identifies three factors that explain the inclusion of sports in the world's cultures:

> In the beginning, sport was a religious cult and a preparation for life. Its roots were in man's desire to gain victory over foes seen and unseen, to influence the forces of nature, and to promote fertility among his crops and cattle.
>
> Sport, as a word, is an abbreviation: the shortened form of disport, a diversion and an amusement. Rooted in Latin, it literally means "carry away" (from *des-porto*).

Travelers to the world's archeological sites are exposed to the pervasiveness of sports throughout the continents and extending back into prehistory. A 4,000-year-old bronze statue excavated from a Mesopotamian temple near Baghdad shows a wrestling scene. Stylized murals on the walls of Mediterranean buildings at Knossos on the Greek island of Crete reveal the presence of boxing in the Minoan civilization. The pharaohs of ancient Egypt would have agreed with sociologist Robert Lynd's contention that "almost any game with any ball is a good game." Balls made of linen or soft leather were often found in excavations of early Egyptian graves. Across the Atlantic, hard rubber balls used centuries ago by the Mayans have been found at sites in Mexico's Yucatan Peninsula.

Physical evidence abounds of athletic contests in antiquity. A traveler's guide to such sites would include such well-known structures as the Coliseum, Rome's oldest standing building; the Hippodrome of the Byzantine Empire in Istanbul; the Mayan ball court near Uxmal in the Yucatan; and the ruins at Olympia in Greece where the first Olympic Games were held in 776 B.C.

The origins of individual sports are many and often difficult to determine. Hundreds of claimants from diverse locations could seek credit for such universal pursuits as archery, fencing, hunting, mountaineering and rock-climbing, rowing and sailing, skiing, soccer, and swimming. Horse racing has undoubtedly existed since the domestication of the first horses, but its development can be traced to the nomadic tribes of Central Asia. British navigator Captain James Cook and his men were the first Europeans to observe the sport of surfing when they sailed to the Hawaiian Islands in 1778. The Native Americans of what would later become Canada and the United States developed lacrosse. Judo traces its origins to China and Japan and karate to Okinawa. Basketball, the only major competitive sport developed in the United States, was invented by Presbyterian minister Dr. James A. Naismith and first played in 1891 at the Springfield, Massachusetts, YMCA. Baseball's origins are cloudy; Abner Doubleday is generally credited with inventing the game, but some detractors claim that, in fact, the game was derived from an English sport called *rounders*.

> **"Baseball is too much of a sport to be a business and too much of a business to be a sport."**
>
> *Philip K. Wrigley (1894–1977)*
> *American executive and owner, Chicago Cubs*

The Business of Sports

The adventure, challenge, and relaxation that have characterized the history of sports continue into the twenty-first century. But a new ingredient has been added to the recipe: money. The management of games and activities most often played by adolescents and young adults matured over time and, largely during the twentieth century, sports became a business.

In a sense, though, sports have always been businesslike. After all, businesses are merely activities and enterprises providing goods and services to clients, customers, fans, patients, parishioners, and other publics. In reality, the only major difference between the Notre Dame University athletic department and Nike Inc. lies with the specific objectives of the two organizations. Nike focuses on profits, revenues, and market share. Notre Dame, like other institutions of higher education, is a not-for-profit organization.

The similarities, however, are more striking than are the differences between the two entities. Both employ highly structured organizations to conduct activities aimed at accomplishing preset objectives. Both seek to serve specific markets and both employ the tools of modern organizations: human resources, finance, production, marketing, and information. Both develop and implement plans and attempt to adhere to budgets. Both recruit highly qualified personnel, and both are effective marketers. In 1990, Notre Dame made a previously unprecedented move by a single institution when it sold the television rights to the football team's six annual home games to NBC Sports. The $1.5 million-per-game agreement, which was recently extended through 2010, is analogous to PepsiCo's Gatorade sports drink collecting added revenues by charging a licensing fee for the use of its name and logo on sports attire.

Components of the Sports Environment

The financial numbers are also similar for the three components of the world of sports:

- Athletes—individuals and organizations engaged in sports activities
- Sporting goods companies—firms supplying goods and services to these individuals and organizations
- Sports media—print and electronic (radio, television, and Internet) media and other companies using sports to market their goods and services

Each component plays a major role in the sports environment of the twenty-first century.

Athletes

The fortunate few who excel at sports enjoy fame, personal satisfaction, and lucrative financial rewards. The approximately 700 major league baseball players currently earn average salaries of one million dollars annually and at least two superstars (outfielder Manny Ramirez and shortstop Alex Rodriguez) command annual contracts of $20 million or more. Such contracts pale in comparison with the NBA, where the average salary exceeds $4.5 million and as recently as 2004, six superstars had contracts of $100 million or more. Tennis typically produces the highest-paid female athletes. And when product endorsement fees, personal appearances, and other secondary revenues are added, the income numbers multiply for most atheletes.

In order of endorsement fees earned, a recent list of the top earning athletes, included the following: Tiger Woods (golf), Michael Jordan (basketball), Kobe Bryant (basketball), Anna Kournikova (tennis), Lance Armstrong (cycling), Shaquille O'Neal (basketball), Venus and Serena Williams (tennis), Barry Bonds (baseball), Tony Hawk (extreme skateboarding), and recent high-school grad

LeBron James (basketball). Nike, Inc. leads in emphasizing product endorsements by sports celebrities In 2003 alone, Nike spent $1.4 billion on endorsement payments to star athletes and sports teams.

During the mid-1990s, basketball superstar Michael Jordan took first place among athlete-endorsers with $13.2 million in income on top of his basic Chicago Bulls' paycheck, and as recently as 2004, he still ranked fourth with $35 million in endorsement fees. Arguably the most successful of the athlete-endorsers is Arnold Palmer.

> "There are two kinds of artists left: those who endorse Pepsi and those who simply won't."
>
> *Annie Lennox (b. 1954) Scottish-born singer*

Sports historians trace sports and entertainment celebrities endorsing consumer products back to Mark McCormack, a lawyer and college friend of Palmer; McCormack negotiated the golf legend's first endorsements during the late 1970s. These early successes led McCormack to form Cleveland-based IMG Sports Management in 1980, the world's foremost private sports management firm. Today the company has offices in major cities around the globe and continues to grow rapidly, despite McCormack's untimely death in 2003.

Palmer, whose total career earnings on the PGA Tour are less than $3 million, garnered endorsement income of $9 million in 2004 from more than 80 international licensees. Despite the three decades that have elapsed since his last PGA victory, Palmer's cadre of corporate sponsors continue to use him as spokesperson because of his immediate recognition, charm, and the fact that they—and their customers—make up a large percentage of the people who play golf, attend golfing events, and watch golf on television.

But striking changes have occurred during the past decade. In 1995, no female athletes earned sufficient income to even make the Top 40. By contrast, the new Top 20 list includes Venus and Serena Williams and Anna Kournikova. Despite an injury-plagued career that has resulted in no singles titles since joining the tour in 1995, Kournikova earns about $15 million a year in endorsements from such international corporations as adidas, Omega watches, and Multiway Sports Bras. But the Russian-born beauty is a favorite of teen boys and twentysomethings and, according to her agent, is more icon than athlete.

Surprisingly, football and hockey stars are noticeably absent from the current list while top earners have emerged from niche sports like cycling and extreme skateboarding. Even more surprising is the initial appearance of LeBron James, a young basketball player who never even won a college—much less an NBA—game, but moved directly from an Akron high school to the NBA's Cleveland Cavaliers.

The price tags on these endorsements are staggering. For donning Nike shoes, LeBron James is paid $90 million. Other deals with Sprite, Powerade and Upper

Deck Trading Cards push his endorsement income above the $100 million mark—even before he first took the court as a member of the Cavaliers. Even the Super Bowl Most Valuable Player who answers the end-of-game "What's Next" question with "I'm going to Disney World" is usually rewarded with $50,000.

Tennis players and golfers tend to be in greatest demand as product endorsers for two reasons. Firstly, their sports attract affluent audiences, particularly young star athletes, such as 28-year-old golf sensation Tiger Woods and the tennis stars who average 19 or 20 years of age. Included among Woods' endorsements are American Express, Accenture, Buick, EA Sports, Nike, Rolex, Tag Huer, Target, and Titleist.

An important second factor is that their reputations have not been tarnished with substance abuse or other legal problems that have plagued basketball and football. Despite ranking third on the most recent list, Kobe Bryant's future product endorsement prospects will be determined by his sexual assault lawsuit.

Sporting-Goods Firms

A second high-dollar component of today's sports world consists of businesses that provide goods and services to athletes, both professional and amateur, talented and inept. The sporting-goods market accounts for sales of about $70 billion a year. Included in this total are sports equipment, exercise machines, footwear, apparel, and sports transportation products such as recreational vehicles and water scooters.

Industry sales have benefited from the fact that casual, sporty dress has become increasingly fashionable; consequently athletic footwear sales are growing at more than 10 percent a year. The sporting goods industry generates $20 billion annually from such sports apparel as sweat suits, spandex pants, and tennis attire, almost as much as the $25 billion produced from the sale of sporting equipment. (The largest subcategories of sporting equipment are exercise equipment, golf equipment, firearms and hunting, camping, and fishing.) Footwear adds another $9 billion to the total. Since most people who buy these jock shoes and jock clothing aren't jocks, it should not be surprising that almost one billion dollars was spent this year on product endorsements by athletes. The linkage of a brand with a sports celebrity is often the determining factor in a sale.

Sports Media

Newspapers, magazines, Internet sites, radio, and television, which includes the networks, cable channels and emerging superstations, provide everything from niche channels devoted exclusively to golf, fitness, rebroadcasts of classic games, women's sports, fee-based sports broadcasts of live baseball, football, basketball—even cricket. Thus an incredible array of news and entertainment is offered to large audiences: readers, listeners, and viewers. In turn, these audiences enable the media to attract advertisers who pay inordinate sums for exposure of their advertising messages. Sports has become one of the most successful areas of programming in terms of advertising, thereby creating a strong environment for competition.

The numbers are staggering. NBC paid $600 million for four years of exclusive broadcast television rights to carry NBA games; CBS paid $1 billion to broadcast the NCAA college basketball tournament for a seven-year period and another $1.1 billion on a four-year contract to televise major league baseball games. The ESPN cable sports network signed a four-year $400 million contract with major league baseball and a similar agreement with the NFL. These huge outlays produce major benefits for both sports franchises and their players. Television rights add at least $15 million annually for each of the 30 major league baseball teams. More than $5.5 million flow into the coffers of each NBA club from television revenue, 53 percent of which is divided among the players.

> **"I always turn to the sports pages first, which record people's accomplishments. The front page has nothing but man's failures."**
>
> *Earl Warren (1891–1974) chief justice of the U.S. Supreme Court*

For sports fans the result is more sports options than ever before, with network sports broadcasters competing with cable sports channels, sports magazines, and even daily sports newspapers. Media management is gambling that the huge outlays will pay off in attracting audiences and advertisers. The 2004 Super Bowl telecast illustrated the fulfillment of their objectives: would-be advertisers anted up $2.5 million for each 30- second commercial.

The Great Sports Quotations

A casual visitor to any one of the nation's bookstores is confronted with an undeniable fact: The reading public likes to read about sports. Dozens of biographies, collections of anecdotes, sports anthologies, scouting reports, and sports quotations comprise a major section of the typical bookstore. But *The Best Things Anybody Ever Said About Sports, Management, and Marketing* represents a first: Until now, all collections of sports quotations have limited their coverage to an alphabetical listing of sports—from auto racing to yachting. No one has ever produced a book focusing on the broader conception of sports as a business and on the components of that business.

Organization of the Book

Unlike the traditional approach of developing an alphabetical list of topics and then inserting quotations under each topic, the organization of *The Best Things Anybody Ever Said About Sports, Management, and Marketing* is based on a logical progression of subjects. The book begins with an introductory section extolling the joy of sports from many perspectives: fans, players, managers, owners, and the other components of the world of sports. These participants are examined in detail in Part Two's six chapters, with individual chapters focusing on players; managers and coaches; fans; sports officials; sportscasters, reporters, and the media; and owners, agents, and attorneys.

"I quote others only the better to express myself."

Michel de Montaigne (1533–1592)
French essayist

The art and science of sports management and marketing is the subject of Part Three. Here the universal management topics of strategies, goals, leadership, motivation, communications, and decision making are featured within the context of sports. This is followed by a three-chapter section titled "Building a Competitive Team." Topics included in this part include the organization; training and conditioning; and winning and losing.

Part Five examines the myriad factors influencing the management and marketing of the twenty-first century athlete. Separate chapters are included on education; the opposite sex (and other distractions); rookies and veterans; and the aging athlete. "Keys to Success in Sports" is the title of Part Six, which includes chapters on team production; sports marketing; money; and records, results, and statistics. The final section, "A Broader Perspective," examines such societal issues as ethics in sports and efforts to create a color-blind sports world.

Choosing Great Sports Quotations

Our objective was to provide the best and most complete collection of quotations ever assembled that relate to the art and science of sports and its management. As a result, the reader will find an interspersing of quotations from sports notables with remarks from political leaders, educators, comedians, war heroes, and well-known CEOs. All of them offer commentary, advice, and experiences to the world of sports and to the participants and organizations involved.

The reader of *The Best Things Anybody Ever Said About Sports, Management, and Marketing* will use the book again and again in one or more ways. Quotations will be chosen for inclusion in speeches, reports, or other written communication. Inevitably, many will be repeated in conversation to add emphasis to discussion topics. To facilitate their use, information is included in the quotation about the author to add context to the point being made. The dates of birth and death as well as a brief description of each author provides insights into the era in which the person being quoted lived and his or her nationality and chief occupation.

In addition to specific sports management and marketing topics, most quotations included in the book contain a considerable element of humor. Moreover, the focus is on quotations that can be told orally or in writing without the need to convert them to 21st century language.

Acknowledgments

We are indebted to many individuals and institutions for invaluable assistance in gathering much of the materials that appear in this book. Special thanks go to the Mobile Public Library, the University of South Alabama Library, and the University of Arkansas Library for their wonderful staffs. We are particularly grateful for our research assistants, Sonni Denver, Colleen Keleher, Tanya McGowan, Jeffrey Price, and Carole Stamps, for their efforts. We can never fully express our appreciation to our research associates, Jeanne Bartimus and Mikhele Taylor, for their many contributions.

LOUIS E. BOONE
DAVID L. KURTZ

ABOUT THE AUTHORS

Few authors have made a greater impact on America's business education during the past three decades than **Louis E. Boone** and **David L. Kurtz**. Since *Contemporary Marketing* first appeared in print in 1974, more than 6 million students have begun their business education by using it or its companion text, *Contemporary Business,* in their classes. A Russian-language version of the latter book serves as the centerpiece of a newly created business education program in the former Soviet Union and translations are available in Chinese, French, Indonesian, Polish, and Portuguese. Both books have received the prestigious McGuffey Award for Textbook Excellence and Longevity. Boone and Kurtz are the only authors ever to write No. 1 texts in two separate business subjects.

Boone, Emeritus Professor of Business and Marketing at the University of South Alabama, was born in Robertsdale, Alabama, and grew up on the Gulf Coast. In addition to his texts, computer simulation games, and scholarly articles, he is author of *Quotable Business,* one of four books on public speaking recommended by *U.S. News & World Report* as "indispensable in any debate." His teaching career has included marketing positions at the University of Arkansas, University of Tulsa, University of Central Florida, University of Southern

Mississippi, Auburn University and international assignments in Australia, Greece, and the United Kingdom.

Boone is an avid collector of more than the ideas of others. His collection of Barbizon art, now part of the permanent collection of the Mobile Museum of Art, is among the finest in the United States. He currently lives with his wife in Mobile, Alabama, where he is a long-suffering Cleveland Indians fan.

Dave Kurtz and Gene Boone became friends and future collaborators as classmates in the University of Arkansas doctoral program. Kurtz was born in Riverside, New Jersey, and grew up on the Eastern Shore of Maryland. He has taught at Seattle University, Eastern Michigan University, Davis & Elkins College, and Australia's Monash University, and currently holds an endowed university professorship at the University of Arkansas.

Kurtz is a prolific researcher and writer. He has authored or coauthored more than 100 books and 130 articles, cases, and papers. He has also been the editor of academic journals, served as president of the Western Marketing Educators Association and vice president of the Academy of Marketing Science. In addition, he served as co-chair of an AMS World Marketing Congress in Melbourne, Australia.

Kurtz currently lives with his wife (and two Yorkies named Daisy and Lucy) in Rogers, Arkansas, where he bleeds Razorback Red and White when it comes to college sports. Ever an optimist, Kurtz also thinks his beloved Seattle Mariners will make it to the World Series during his lifetime.

Part I

Introduction

Chapter 1

The Joy of Sports

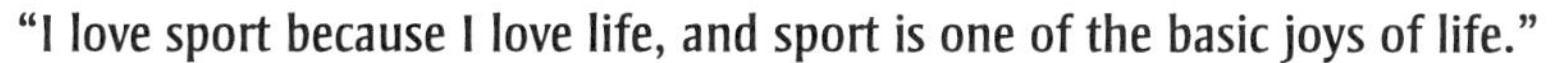

"I love sport because I love life, and sport is one of the basic joys of life."

Yevgeny Yevtushenko (b. 1933)
Russian author and poet

"Sports is the toy department of human life."

Howard Cosell (1920–1995)
American sportscaster and author

"Almost any game with any ball is a good game."

Robert Lynd (1892–1950)
American sociologist

"The invention of basketball was not an accident. It was developed to meet a need. Those boys simply would not play Drop the Handkerchief."

Dr. James Naismith (1861–1939)
American minister and athletic director
(inventor of basketball)

"If a man watches three football games in a row, he should be declared legally dead."

Erma Bombeck (1927–1996)
American writer and humorist

"That's the true harbinger of spring, not crocuses or swallows returning to Capistrano, but the sound of a bat on a ball."

Bill Veeck (1914–1986)
American baseball team owner

"When life is suddenly more serious more of the time, there is also more need for it to be fun at least some of the time. That's why my family will be at a college football game this weekend. We need it. And deserve it, too. Not like a New York fireman deserves it. Or a medic at the Pentagon. But enough."

Thomas Boswell
Washington Post *sports columnist*
(on his family's weekend plans following the 9/11 terrorist attacks)

"The first big-league game I ever saw was at the Polo Grounds. My father took me. I remember it so well: the green grass and the green stands. It was like seeing Oz."

John Curtis (b. 1948)
American professional baseball player

"Two things only the people anxiously desire: bread and the circus games."

Juvenal (c.55–c.127)
(Decimus Junius Juvenalis)
Roman satirical poet

"Baseball is a game where a curve is an optical illusion, a screwball can be a pitch or a person, stealing is legal, and you can spit anywhere you like except in the umpire's eye or on the ball."

Jim Murray (1919–2003)
American sports columnist

"It breaks your heart. It is designed to break your heart. The game begins in the spring, when everything else begins again, and it blossoms in the summer, filling the afternoons and evenings, and then as soon as the chill rains come, it stops and leaves you to face the fall alone."

A. Bartlett Giamatti (1938–1989)
American educator and major league baseball commissioner

"Here is a game in which there is no clock, the defense holds the ball, though it has rigid rules, every park is different, the greatest heroes fail seven times out of ten, a game that's born in the spring, dies in the fall. This is life."

Kenneth L. Burns (b. 1953)
American documentary filmmaker

"Baseball, to me, is still the national pastime because it is a summer game. I feel that almost all Americans are summer people, that summer is what they think of when they think of their childhood. I think it stirs up an incredible emotion within people."

Steve Busby (b. 1948)
American professional baseball player

"Life is good, but basketball is better."

Lou Carnesecca (b. 1925)
former St. John's University head basketball coach

"Being on the tightrope is living; everything else is waiting."

Karl Wallenda (1905–1978)
American aerialist and circus performer

"I do much of my creative thinking while golfing. If people know you are working at home they think nothing of walking in for a coffee. But they wouldn't dream of interrupting you on the golf course."

Harper Lee (b. 1926)
American author

"The golf course is the only place I can go dressed like a pimp and fit in perfectly. Anywhere else, lime-green pants and alligator shoes . . ."

Samuel L. Jackson (b. 1948)
American actor

"If you watch a game, it's fun. If you play it, it's recreation. If you work at it, it's golf."

Bob Hope (1903–2003)
American actor and comedian

"Golf is like life in a lot of ways. All the biggest wounds are self-inflicted."

Bill Clinton (b. 1946)
42nd president of the United States (1993–2001)

"It took my 17 years to get three thousand hits in baseball. I did it in one afternoon on the golf course."

Hank Aaron (b. 1934)
American professional baseball player

"Golf has humbled, humiliated, and just about licked every great athlete I ever knew who tried it."

Red Blaik (1897–1989)
head football coach, U.S. Military Academy

"In golf, humiliations are the essence of the game."

Alistair Cooke (1908–2004)
American journalist and broadcaster

"A noted psychiatrist's wife asked him why he never let her play golf with him. "My dear," he admonished her, "there are three things a man must do alone: testify, die, and putt."

Bennett Cerf (1898–1971)
American editor, publisher, and author

"Golf is a good walk spoiled."

Mark Twain (1835–1910)
American author

"I play in the low 80s. If it's any hotter than that, I won't play."

Joe E. Lewis (1902–1971)
American comedian

"I deny allegations by Bob Hope that during my last game [of golf] I hit an eagle, a birdie, an elk, and a moose."

Gerald R. Ford (b. 1913)
38th president of the United States (1974–1977)
(who was well-known for his erratic drives)

"My swing is so bad I look like a caveman killing his lunch."

Lee Trevino (b. 1939)
American professional golfer

"The only reason I ever played golf in the first place was so I could afford to hunt and fish."

Sam Snead (1912–2002)
American professional golfer

"When a man wants to murder a tiger he calls it sport; when a tiger wants to murder him he calls it ferocity."

George Bernard Shaw (1856–1950)
British playwright and social reformer

"A dead bird or animal is dead. The light gone from the radiant eye, the rainbow sheen instantly drying off fur and feather, the rot begun the moment of death. And there was no beauty in it."

Unknown

"Bullfighting is the only art in which the artist is in danger of death and in which the degree of brilliance in the performance is left to the fighter's honor."

Ernest Hemingway (1898–1961)
American author

"Serious sport has nothing to do with fair play. It is bound up with hatred, jealousy, boastfulness, disregard of all rules and sadistic pleasure in witnessing violence. In other words it is war minus the shooting."

George Orwell (1903–1950)
British author

"To say that politics is not a part of sports is not being realistic. When I run, I am more than a runner. I am a diplomat, an ambassador for my country."

Filbert Bayi
Tanzanian distance runner
(in 1974, the first person to run the mile in under 3:50.)

"Wild animals never kill for sport. Man is the only one to whom the torture and death of his fellow creatures is amusing in itself."

James A. Froude (1818–1894)
British historian

"It is veneer, rouge, aestheticism, art museums, new theaters, etc., that make America important. The good things are football, kindness, and jazz bands."

George Santayana (1863–1952)
American poet and philosopher

"You can't be a real country unless you have a beer and an airline—it helps if you have some kind of a football team, or some nuclear weapons, but at the very least you need a beer."

Frank Zappa (1940–1993)
former lead singer, The Mothers of Invention

"Whoever wants to know the heart and mind of America had better learn baseball."

Jacques Barzun (b. 1907)
American educator

"America is good at three things: basketball, making war, and buying stuff."

Watts Wacker
American futurist, author, and chairman, FirstMatter

"It's clear that God is a baseball fan. Right there in the first verse of the Bible it says, 'In the big inning, God created heaven and earth.'"

Anonymous

"Don't tell me about the world. Not today. It's springtime and they're knocking baseballs around fields where the grass is damp and green in the morning and the kids are trying to hit the curve ball."

Pete Hamill (b. 1935)
American sportswriter

"At its best, sport is living drama."

John Bromley (b. 1937)
English writer

"If all the year were playing holidays, to sport would be as tedious as to work."

William Shakespeare (1564–1616)
English dramatist and poet

“The game is my *wife*. It demands loyalty and responsibility, and it gives me back fulfillment and peace.”

Michael Jordan (b. 1963)
American professional basketball player

“Don’t *worry* about it. It’s just a bunch of guys with an odd-shaped ball.”

Bill Parcells (b. 1941)
American professional football coach

“Watching Carl Lewis run against his countrymen is little short of boring. But put him, as an American, in a race against the rest of the world, and suddenly everything changes.”

Richard W. Pound (b. 1942)
American International Olympic Committee member

“One way to stop a runaway horse is to bet on him.”

Toronto Globe and Mail

“Football is violence and cold weather and sex and college rye. Horse racing is animated roulette. Boxing is smoky halls and kidneys battered until they bleed. Tennis and golf are best played, not watched. Basketball, hockey, and track meets are action heaped upon action, climax upon climax, until the onlooker’s responses become deadened. Baseball is for the leisurely afternoons of summer and for the unchanging dreams.”

Roger Kahn (b. 1927)
American author

“Football is, after all, a wonderful way to get rid of aggressions without going to jail for it.”

Heywood Hale Broun (1888–1955)
American journalist

“It’s a very interesting game. They have big bears up front and little rabbits in the back. The idea is for the bears to protect the rabbits.”

Viktor Tikonov
Russian hockey coach
(on observing his first American football game)

"Football features two of the worst parts of American life—violence punctuated by committee meetings."

George F. Will (b. 1941)
American news commentator and author

"Next to religion, baseball has furnished a greater impact on American life than any other institution."

Herbert Hoover (1874–1964)
31st president of the United States (1929–1933)

"I was born for soccer, just as Beethoven was born for music."

Edson Arantes Do Nascimento (Pelé) (b. 1940)
Brazilian soccer star

"Anyone who will tear down sports will tear down America. Sports and religion have made America what it is today."

Woody Hayes (1913–1987)
American college football coach

"Sports must be amateur or it is not sport. Sports played professionally are entertainment."

Avery Brundage (1887–1975)
American International Olympic Committee president

"The America's Cup is as exciting as watching grass grow."

Ringold "Ring" Lardner (1885–1933)
American sportswriter and author

"Clemson will never subsidize a sport where a man sits on his tail and goes backward."

Frank Howard (b. 1936)
American university athletic director
(explaining his decision not to include crew as a varsity sport at Clemson University)

"One of the advantages bowling has over golf is that you very seldom lose a bowling ball."

Don Carter (b. 1926)
American bowling champion

"The sport of skiing consists of wearing three thousand dollars' worth of clothes and equipment and driving two hundred miles in the snow in order to stand around at a bar and get drunk."

P.J. O'Rourke (b. 1945)
American writer

"Skiing: the art of catching cold and going broke while rapidly heading nowhere at great personal risk."

Anonymous

"Skiing combines outdoor fun with knocking down trees with your face."

Dave Barry (b. 1947)
American newspaper columnist

"I'd give up golf if I didn't have so many sweaters."

Bob Hope (1903–2003)
American actor and comedian

"If it weren't for golf, I'd be waiting on this table instead of sitting at it."

Judy Rankin (b. 1945)
American professional golfer

"The golf course is the greatest office in the world—six miles of fresh air."

Chi Chi Rodriguez (b. 1935)
Puerto Rican professional golfer

"Major league baseball has done as much as any one thing in this country to keep up the spirit of the people."

Franklin D. Roosevelt (1882–1945)
32nd president of the United States (1933–1945)

"You gotta be a man to play baseball for a living but you gotta have a lot of little boy in you, too."

Roy Campanella (1921–1993)
American professional baseball player

"To see some of our best-educated boys spending the afternoon knocking each other down while thousands cheer them on hardly gives a picture of a peace-loving nation."

Lyndon B. Johnson (1908–1973)
36th president of the United States (1963–1969)

"Football is not a contact sport—it's a collision sport. Dancing is a contact sport."

Vince Lombardi (1913–1970)
American professional football coach

"People stress the violence. That's the smallest part of it. Football is brutal only from a distance. In the middle of it there's a calm, a tranquility. The players accept pain. There's a sense of order even at the end of a running play with bodies strewn everywhere. When the systems interlock, there's a satisfaction to the game that can't be duplicated. There's a harmony."

Don DeLillo (b. 1936)
American author

"What other people may find in poetry or art museums, I find in the flight of a good drive—the white ball sailing up into the blue sky, growing smaller and smaller, then suddenly reaching its apex, curving, falling, and finally dropping to the turf to roll some more, just the way I planned it."

Arnold Palmer (b. 1929)
American professional golfer

"Prizefighting offers a profession to men who might otherwise commit murder in the street."

Norman Mailer (b. 1923)
American author

"I say get an education. Become an electrician, a mechanic, a doctor, a lawyer—anything but a fighter. In this trade, it's the managers that make the money and last the longest."

Muhammad Ali (b. 1942)
American heavyweight boxing champion

NOTICE TO REPORTERS

"You Saw the Game. Take What You Need."

1. "I'm just glad to be here. I just want to help the club any way I can."
2. "Baseball's a funny game."
3. "I'd rather be lucky than good."
4. "We're going to take the season one game at a time."
5. "You're only as good as your last game (last at-bat)."
6. "This game has really changed."
7. "If we stay healthy we should be right there."
8. "It takes 24 (25) players."
9. "We need two more players to take us over the top: Babe Ruth and Lou Gehrig."
10. "We have a different hero every day."
11. "We'll get 'em tomorrow."
12. "This team seems ready to gel."
13. "With a couple breaks, we win that game."
14. "That All-Star voting is a joke."
15. "The catcher and I were on the same wavelength."
16. "I just went right at 'em."
17. "I did my best and that's all I can do."
18. "You just can't pitch behind."
19. "That's the name of the game."
20. "We've got to have fun."
21. "I didn't have my good stuff, but I battled 'em."
22. "Give the guy some credit; he hit a good pitch."
23. "Hey, we were due to catch a break or two."
24. "Yes."
25. "No."
26. "That's why they pay him ___ million dollars."
27. "Even I could hit that pitch."
28. "I know you are but what am I?"
29. "I was getting my off-speed stuff over so they couldn't sit on the fastball."
30. "I have my at-'em ball going today."
31. "I had some great plays made behind me tonight."
32. "I couldn't have done it without my teammates."
33. "You saw it . . . write it."
34. "I just wanted to go as hard as I could as long as I could."
35. "I'm seeing the ball real good."
36. "I hit that ball good."
37. "I don't get paid to hit."

Don Carman (b. 1959)
American professional baseball player
(clichés posted on his locker during the 1990 season)

Chapter 2

Sports Marketing

"The most beautiful thing in the world is a ballpark filled with people."

Bill Veeck (1914–1986)
American baseball team owner

"When I started out, baseball was played by nine tough competitors on grass in graceful ballparks. By the time I was finished, there were ten men on each side, the game was played indoors, on plastic, and I had to spend half of my time watching out for a man dressed in a chicken suit who kept trying to kiss me."

Ron Luciano (1937–1995)
American baseball umpire

"Every day in every way, baseball gets fancier. A few more years and they'll be playing on oriental rugs."

Russell Baker (b. 1925)
American journalist

"Spend whatever it takes to build the best. Then let people know about it. In New York, there is no limit to how much money people will spend for the very best, not second best, the very best."

Donald J. Trump (b. 1946)
American businessman and celebrity

"A baseball team is a commercial venture, operating for a profit. The idea that you don't have to package your product as attractively as General Motors packages its products, and hustle your product the way General Motors hustles its product, is baseball's most pernicious enemy."

Bill Veeck (1914–1986)
American baseball team owner

"The man who uses Calloway golf clubs, drives a Jaguar, and wears Ralph Lauren apparel makes a statement about his identity. He is a man separate and apart from the man who uses a Penn fishing reel, drives a Dodge Durango, and wears Levi's."

Laurence Vincent
American author

"Be it the boardroom or the football field, you've got to cut your burn and drive your revenue."

Troy Vincent (b. 1971)
Philadelphia Eagles cornerback and entrepreneur

"Before you build a better mousetrap, it helps to know if there are any mice out there."

Mortimer B. Zuckerman (b. 1937)
chairman and editor in chief, U.S. News & World Report

"Consumers are statistics. Customers are people."

Stanley Marcus (1905–2002)
American merchant

"Increasingly, the center of the marketing universe is the customer. It's the customer who sets the rules and the marketer who responds."

H. Robert Wientzen (b. 1939)
former president and CEO, Direct Marketing Association

"If you give something worth paying for, they'll pay."

Thomas J. Peters (b. 1932)
American business writer

"When the product is right, you don't have to be a great marketer."

Lee Iacocca (b. 1924)
former chairman, Chrysler Corp.

"Sporting goods companies pay me not to endorse their products."

Bob Uecker (b. 1935)
American baseball player and sportscaster

"I never bought an article of clothing because some famous athlete told me to, but then I never had a diamond in my ear, either."

Jim Murray (1919–2003)
American sports columnist

"You can hype a questionable product for a little while, but you'll never build an enduring business."

Victor Kiam (b. 1926)
Former CEO, Remington Products, Inc. and owner,
New England Patriots professional football team

"American football is an occasion at which dancing girls, bands, tactical huddles, and television commercial breaks are interrupted by short bursts of play."

London Times

"So many sports organizations have built their entire budgets around television that if we ever withdrew the money, the whole structure would collapse."

Roone Arledge (1931–2002)
American sports TV pioneer

"Don't sell the steak, sell the sizzle!"

Elmer Wheeler
Depression-era American salesperson

"Many a small thing has been made large by the right kind of advertising."

Mark Twain (1835–1910)
American author

"Chess: The greatest misuse of human intelligence outside an advertising agency."

Raymond Chandler (1888–1959)
American mystery writer

"If you think advertising doesn't pay—we understand there are 25 mountains in Colorado higher than Pike's Peak. Can you name one?"

The American Salesman

"The most powerful element in advertising is the truth."

William Bernbach (1911–1982)
Founder, Doyle Dane Bernbach advertising agency

"Advertising in the final analysis should be news. If it is not news, it is worthless."

Adolph S. Ochs (1858–1935)
American newspaper publisher

"Never write an advertisement which you wouldn't want your family to read. You wouldn't tell lies to your own wife. Don't tell them to mine. Do as you would be done by. If you tell lies about a product, you will be found out—either by the Government, which will prosecute you, or by the consumer, who will punish you by not buying your product a second time. Good products can be sold by honest advertising. If you don't think the product is good, you have no business to be advertising it."

David M. Ogilvy (1911–1999)
Founder, Ogilvy & Mather advertising agency

"Advertising is the rattling of a stick inside a swill bucket."

George Orwell (1903–1950)
English author

"Doing business without advertising is like winking at a girl in the dark. You know what you are doing, but nobody else does."

Steuart Henderson Britt (1907–1979)
American educator

"Some men go through a forest and see no firewood."

English proverb

"Half the money I spend on advertising is wasted, and the trouble is, I don't know which half."

John Wanamaker (1838–1922)
American merchant

"The codfish lays ten thousand eggs,
The homely hen lays one.
The codfish never cackles
To tell you what she's done.
And so we scorn the codfish,
While the humble hen we prize,
Which only goes to show you
That it pays to advertise."

Anonymous

"Imagination is more important than knowledge."

Albert Einstein (1879–1955)
American physicist

"Everyone lives by selling something."

Robert Louis Stevenson (1850–1894)
Scottish author

"It's no trick to be a successful salesman if you have what the people want. You never hear the bootleggers complaining about hard times."

Robert C. "Bob" Edwards (1864–1954)
Canadian educator and humorist

"Selling focuses on the need of the seller; marketing on the needs of the buyer. Selling is preoccupied with the seller's need to convert his product into cash; marketing with the idea of satisfying the needs of the customer by means of the product and the whole cluster of things associated with the creating, delivering, and finally consuming it."

Theodore Levitt (b. 1925)
American educator and author

"When the one great scorer comes to mark against your name, it's not whether you won or lost but how many paid to see the game."

Peter Bavasi (b. 1942)
American baseball executive (paraphrasing sportswriter Grantland Rice's famous poem)

"Nothing except the mint can make money without advertising."

Thomas B. Macaulay (1800–1859)
English author, historian, and statesman

"We grew up founding our dreams on the infinite promise of American advertising. I still believe that one can learn to play the piano by mail and that mud will give you a perfect complexion."

Zelda Fitzgerald (1900–1948)
American artist, dancer, and writer

"Cutting prices is usually insanity if the competition can go as low as you can."

Michael Porter (b. 1947)
American educator

SEVEN RULES FOR FINDING A PARKING SPACE AT THE BIG GAME

1. The first parking space you see will be the last parking space you see. Grab it.
2. Making eye contact revokes your right of way.
3. Always look both ways before running a red light.
4. Never use directional signals when changing lanes. They only warn other drivers to speed up and not let you in.
5. When on a one-way street, stay to the right to allow oncoming traffic to pass.
6. If a pedestrian ahead of you steps into the street, speed up, honk, or yell obscenities loudly and chase him back up on the curb.
7. Never get in the way of a car that needs extensive bodywork.

Part 2

Participants in the World of Sports

Chapter 3

Players

"Whoever said, 'It's not whether you win or lose that counts,' probably lost."

Martina Navratilova (b. 1956)
American professional tennis player

"Grantland Rice, the great sports writer once said, 'It's not whether you win or lose, it's how you play the game.' Well, Grantland Rice can go to hell as far as I'm concerned."

Gene Autry (1907–1998)
American actor and former owner, California Angels baseball team

"'How you play the game' is for college boys. When you're playing for money, winning is the only thing that matters. Show me a good loser in professional sports, and I'll show you an idiot. Show me a sportsman, and I'll show you a player I'm looking to trade to Oakland."

Leo Durocher (1905–1991)
American baseball player and manager

"Show me a guy who's afraid to look bad, and I'll show you a guy you can beat every time."

Lou Brock (b. 1939)
American professional baseball player

"You can only become a winner if you are willing to walk over the edge."

Ronald E. McNair (1950–1986)
American astronaut
(died in 1986 Challenger *space shuttle explosion)*

"Cowards never started and the weak died along the way."

19th century pioneers reflecting on completing the Oregon Trail

"Everyone has some fear. A man who has no fear belongs in a mental institution. Or on special teams."

Walt Michaels (b. 1929)
American professional football coach

"Football is one-third offense, one-third defense, and one-third special teams."

George Allen (1918–1990)
American college and professional football coach

"There's nothing better in life than a head-on collision."

Lawrence Taylor (b. 1959)
American professional football player

"Like artists and achievers of every kind, successful athletes must be, at a minimum, four things: gifted, hungry, intelligent, and tough-minded."

Edwin H. Cady (b. 1917)
English educator and author

"Champions take responsibility. When the ball is coming over the net, you can be sure I want the ball."

Billie Jean King (b. 1943)
American professional tennis player

"I think I fail a bit less than everyone else."

Jack Nicklaus (b. 1940)
American professional golfer

"When Jack Nicklaus plays well, he wins.
When he plays badly, he finishes second.
When he plays terrible, he finishes third."

Johnny Miller (b. 1947)
American professional golfer

"There isn't enough mustard in the world to cover Reggie Jackson."

Darrold Knowles (b. 1941)
American professional baseball player
(when asked if his former teammate was a hot dog)

"He'd give you the shirt off his back. Of course, he'd call a press conference to announce it."

Jim "Catfish" Hunter (1946–1999)
American professional baseball player
(on Reggie Jackson)

"You have reached the pinnacle of success as soon as you become uninterested in money, compliments, or publicity."

Dr. O.A. Battista (b. 1917)
American chemist

"I'm just a golfer, man. I chase a little white ball around and work on my farmer tan."

Tiger Woods (b. 1975)
American golfer
(in reference to comment about his celebrity status)

"Blind people come to the park just to listen to him pitch."

Reggie Jackson (b. 1946)
American professional baseball player
(on New York Mets pitcher Tom Seaver)

"My only regret in life is that I can't sit in the stands and watch me pitch."

Bo Belinsky (1936–2001)
American professional baseball player

"There have been only two geniuses in the world: Willie Mays and Willie Shakespeare."

Tallulah Bankhead (1903–1968)
American actress

"Trying to sneak a pitch past Hank Aaron is like trying to sneak the sunrise past a rooster."

Curt Simmons (b. 1929)
American professional baseball player

"I don't want to throw him nothin'. Maybe he'll just get tired of waitin' and leave."

Vernon "Lefty" Gomez (1908–1989)
American professional baseball player
(facing hitter Jimmy Foxx and answering catcher Bill Dickey's question, "What do you want to throw him?")

"Cool Papa Bell was so fast he could get out of bed, turn out the lights across the room, and be back in bed under the covers before the lights went out."

Josh Gibson (1911–1947)
American professional baseball player
(on James "Cool Papa" Bell [1903–1991], baseball legend, and, in 1946, Negro Leagues' highest-paid player at $90 a month)

"What counts is not necessarily the size of the dog in the fight—it's the size of the fight in the dog."

Dwight D. Eisenhower (1890–1969)
34th president of the United States (1953–1961)

"You're a hero when you win and a bum when you lose. That's the game."

Johnny Unitas (1933–2003)
American professional football player

"A hero ain't nothing but a sandwich."

Charles Barkley (b. 1963)
American professional basketball player

"He had a God-given killer instinct."

Al Davis (b. 1929)
Owner, Oakland Raiders professional football team
(on quarterback George Blanda)

"There's no way you can have consistent success without players. No one can win without material. But not everyone can win with material."

John Wooden (b. 1910)
American college basketball coach

"Amateurs hope. Professionals work."

Garson Kanin (1912–1999)
American dramatist and theatrical director

"A professional is a man who can do his best at a time when he doesn't particularly feel like it."

Alistair Cooke (1908–2004)
English-born journalist and broadcaster

"The valuable person in any business is the individual who can and will cooperate with others."

Elbert Hubbard (1856–1915)
American writer

"If I ain't startin', I ain't departin'."

Garry Templeton (b. 1956)
American professional baseball player
(on being chosen as a substitute on the All-Star Game roster)

"Baseball players are the weirdest of all. I think it's all that organ music."

Peter Gent (b. 1942)
American writer

"People are not remembered by how few times they fail, but by how often they succeed. Every wrong step is another step forward."

Thomas Edison (1847–1931)
American inventor

"I came; I saw; I got my butt kicked."

Christopher Bowman (b. 1967)
American figure skater
(on a disappointing fourth-place finish in the 1992 Winter Olympics)

"When you're hitting the ball, it comes at you looking like a grapefruit. When you're not, it looks like a black-eyed pea."

George Scott (b. 1944)
American professional baseball player

"If they retired the numbers of all greats at Notre Dame, there wouldn't be any numbers left."

Terry Hanratty (b. 1948)
American football player
(at a ceremony retiring his Notre Dame football number)

"Recruiting is a lot like shaving. You miss a day and you look like a bum."

Jackie Sherrill (b. 1943)
American college football coach

"I want this on my tombstone: 'Pepper Rodgers was a terrible recruiter, but he overcame it with great coaching.'"

Pepper Rodgers (b. 1931)
American college football coach

"We spend too much time recruiting and not enough time working with the players we have."

Alex Agase (b. 1922)
American college football coach

"More than anything, it's whether or not a manager has the horses to go out there and win for him. That's all."

Chuck Cottier (b. 1936)
American baseball manager and coach

"They recruit McDonald's All-Americans. We recruit guys who eat at McDonald's."

Phil Martelli (b. 1954)
American college basketball coach
(on the difference between his program at St. Joseph University and rival University of Arizona)

"It's sort of like a beauty contest. It's very easy to pick the top one, two, or three girls, but then the rest of them look the same. It's like that in scouting."

Gil Brandt
former director of player personnel, Dallas Cowboys

"Doctors bury their mistakes. We still have ours on scholarship."

Abe Lemons (1922–2002)
former University of Texas basketball coach

"Any man who selects a goal in life which can be fully achieved has already defined his own limitations."

Cavett Robert (1907–97)
American writer and speaker

"Sure, luck means a lot in football. Not having a good quarterback is bad luck."

Don Shula (b. 1930)
American professional football coach

"Luck is what happens when preparation meets opportunity."

Darrell K. Royal (b. 1924)
American college football coach and athletic director

"Luck is the residue of design."

Branch Rickey (1881–1965)
American baseball team owner

"I skate to where the puck is going to be, not where it has been."

Wayne Gretsky (b. 1961)
Canadian professional hockey player

"We take the shortest route to the puck and arrive in ill humor."

Bobby Clarke (b. 1949)
National Hockey League player and executive

"An athlete who walks in another's tracks leaves no footprints."

Anonymous

"Everything comes to him who hustles while he waits."

Thomas Edison (1847–1931)
American inventor

"Glory is fleeting, but obscurity is forever."

Napoleon Bonaparte (1769–1821)
Emperor of France (1804–1815)

"In the future everyone will be famous for fifteen minutes."

Andy Warhol (1928–1987)
American artist and filmmaker

"Publicity is like poison: it doesn't hurt unless you swallow."

Joe Paterno (b. 1926)
American college football coach

"The average athlete thinks he isn't."

Anonymous

"I'm no different from anybody else with two arms, two legs, and 4,200 hits."

Pete Rose (b. 1941)
American professional baseball player

"I don't want people to forget Babe Ruth. I just want them to remember Henry Aaron."

Hank Aaron (b. 1934)
American professional baseball player
(on breaking the Babe's record for home runs)

"It's really impossible for athletes to grow up. As long as you're playing, no one will let you. On the one hand, you're a child, still playing a game. And everybody around you acts like a kid, too. But on the other hand, you're a superhuman hero that everyone dreams of being. No wonder we have such a hard time understanding who we are."

Billie Jean King (b. 1943)
American professional tennis player

"In heaven an angel is nobody in particular."

George Bernard Shaw (1856–1950)
British author and social reformer

"Everybody looks good on paper."

John Y. Brown (b. 1933)
American executive and former governor of Kentucky

"The worst curse in life is 'unlimited potential.'"

Ken Brett (1948–2003)
American professional baseball player

"The only thing worse than being talked about is not being talked about."

Oscar Wilde (1854–1900)
Irish poet, playwright, and novelist

"You have to have a nickname to be remembered."

James Lamar "Dusty" Rhodes (b. 1927)
American professional baseball player
(whose record 4 home runs made the San Francisco utility player the hero of the 1954 World Series)

"I refuse to call a 52-year-old man Sparky."

Al Clark
American baseball umpire
(on his insistence in 1986 on calling the Detroit Tigers manager "George Anderson")

"What's in a name? That which we call a rose
By any other name would smell as sweet."

William Shakespeare (1564–1616)
English dramatist and poet

"My father is an undertaker, and I worked for him part-time. There were certain advantages to the job. For instance, while I was dating my wife I sent her flowers every day."

Richard "Digger" Phelps (b. 1940)
American college basketball coach
(on the origin of his nickname)

"Father calls me William, sister calls me Will,
Mother calls me Willie, but the fellows call me Bill!"

Eugene Field (1850–1895)
American poet and journalist

"Every time I sign a ball, and there have been thousands, I thank my luck that I wasn't born Coveleski, or Wambsganss, or Peckinpaugh."

Mel Ott (1909–1959)
American professional baseball player

"Canada is a country whose main exports are hockey players and cold fronts. Our main imports are baseball players and acid rain."

Pierre Trudeau (1919–2000)
Prime Minister of Canada (1968–1979; 1980–1984)

"There are only five things you can do in baseball: run, throw, catch, hit, and hit with power."

Leo Durocher (1905–1991)
American baseball player and manager

"He can't hit, he can't run, he can't field, he can't throw. He can't do a goddam thing . . . but beat you."

Branch Rickey (1881–1965)
American professional baseball club owner
(on baseball player Eddie Stankey)

"Good pitching always stops good hitting and vice versa."

Casey Stengel (1891–1975)
American baseball manager

"He was something like 0 for 21 the first time I saw him. His first major league hit was a home run off me—and I'll never forgive myself. We might have gotten rid of Willie forever if I'd only struck him out."

Warren Spahn (1921–2003)
American professional baseball player
(on Willie Mays)

"To achieve anything in this game, you must be prepared to dabble on the boundary of disaster."

Stirling Moss (b. 1929)
British auto racing champion

"In my book a tennis player is the complete athlete. He has to have the speed of a sprinter, the endurance of a marathon runner, the agility of a boxer or fencer, and the gray matter of a good football quarterback. Baseball, football, basketball players are good athletes, but they don't need all these attributes to perform well."

Bobby Riggs (1918–1995)
American professional tennis player

"Some people try to find things in this game that don't exist, but football is only two things—blocking and tackling."

Vince Lombardi (1913–1970)
American professional football coach

"In 26 years in the pros, I haven't noticed many changes. The players are faster, bigger, smarter, and more disloyal to their owners, but that's about it."

George Blanda (b. 1927)
American professional football player

"The man who complains about the way the ball bounces is likely the one who dropped it."

Lou Holtz (b. 1937)
American college football coach

"You don't play people. You play a ball. You don't ever hit a guy in the butt and knock him over the net—unless you're really upset."

Vic Braden (b. 1929)
American tennis instructor

"It has always been my private conviction that any man who pits his intelligence against a fish and loses has it coming."

John Steinbeck (1902–1968)
American novelist

"It is to be observed that 'angling' is the name given to fishing by people who can't fish."

Stephen Leacock (1869–1944)
Canadian economist and humorist

"If fishing is a religion, fly fishing is high church."

Tom Brokaw (b. 1940)
American newscaster and author

"Fly fishing may be a very pleasant amusement; but angling or float fishing I can only compare to a stick and a string, with a worm at one end and a fool at the other."

Samuel Johnson (1709–1784)
English lexicographer and author

"Any game where a man 60 can beat a man 30 ain't no game."

Burt Shotten (1884–1962)
American baseball manager
(on golf)

"I guess he's a nice guy, but a golfer isn't an athlete. I could take up golf and do a lot better at it than any golfer could do taking up fighting, I guarantee you. I don't understand these people that vote."

Joe Frazier (b. 1944)
World heavyweight boxing champion, 1970–1973
(on learning golfer Lee Trevino was voted Athlete of the Year)

FAVORITE SPORTS NICKNAMES

Players

1. George "The Iceman" Gervin
2. William "The Refrigerator" Perry
3. Dennis "Oil Can" Boyd
4. "Three Fingers" Brown
5. Alan "The Horse" Ameche
6. Elroy "Crazy Legs" Hirsch
7. Deion "Prime Time" Sanders
8. Willie "Puddin' Head" Jones
9. Kenny "The Snake" Stabler
10. Clint "Scrap Iron" Courtney

Colleges

1. UC Santa Cruz Banana Slugs
2. Oglethorpe Stormy Petrels
3. Arkansas Tech Wonderboys
4. UC Irvine Anteaters
5. Northern Montana Northern Lights
6. Evergreen State Geoducks
7. Indiana University/Purdue University Mastodons
8. Washburn University Ichabods
9. Heidelburg College Student Princes
10. Lincoln Memorial Railsplitters

Chapter 4

Managers and Coaches

"I'll tell you what makes a great manager: a great manager has a knack for making ballplayers think they are better than they think they are. He forces you to have a good opinion of yourself. He lets you know he believes in you. He makes you get more out of yourself. And once you learn how good you really are, you never settle for playing anything less than your very best."

Reggie Jackson (b. 1946)
American professional baseball player

"Business is about managing people, and the lessons of a coach can definitely be applied to a CEO."

Lisa Delpy Neirotti
Professor of sports management at George Washington University

"Managing is getting paid for home runs someone else hits."

Casey Stengel (1891–1975)
American baseball manager

"If the coach cannot do it, he cannot teach it—only talk about it."

Percy Cerutty (1895–1975)
Australian track coach

"Being in politics is like being a football coach. You have to be smart enough to understand the game and dumb enough to think it's important."

Eugene McCarthy (b. 1916)
United States Senator (1958–1970)

"I never made the [football] team. I was not heavy enough to play the line, not fast enough to play halfback, and not smart enough to be quarterback."

Richard M. Nixon (1913–1994)
37th president of the United States (1969–1974)

"Most pitchers are too smart to manage."

Jim Palmer (b. 1945)
American professional baseball player

"They X-rayed my head and found nothing."

Jay Hanna "Dizzy" Dean (1910–1974)
American pitcher

"The secret of successful managing is to keep the five guys who hate you away from the five guys who haven't made up their minds."

Casey Stengel (1891–1975)
American baseball manager

"Some coaches pray for wisdom. I pray for 260-pound tackles."

Chuck Mills (b. 1928)
American college football coach

"Any manager who can't get along with a .400 hitter ought to have his head examined."

Joe McCarthy (1887–1978)
American baseball manager
(on managing Ted Williams)

"I tell him, 'Attaway to hit, George.'"

Jim Frey (b. 1931)
American baseball manager
(on how he advised Kansas City Royals hitting star George Brett)

"Eagles don't flock—you have to find them one at a time."

H. Ross Perot (b. 1930)
American computer industry executive and philanthropist

"We take eagles and teach them to fly in formation."

D. Wayne Calloway (b. 1935)
former CEO, PepsiCo Inc.

"In American society, it is commonly accepted that the success or failure of an athlete unit depends almost entirely upon the competence or incompetence of its coach."

Harry Edwards (b. 1942)
American sociologist

"Coaching is nothing more than eliminating mistakes before you get fired."

Lou Holtz (b. 1937)
American football coach

"Call me arrogant, cocky, crybaby, whiner, and whatever names you like. At least they're not calling us losers anymore. If people like you, it's probably because they're beating you."

Steve Spurrier (b. 1945)
American college and professional football coach

"Coaching is easy. Winning is the hard part."

Elgin Baylor (b. 1934)
American basketball player and coach

"A coach isn't as smart as they say he is when he wins, or as stupid when he loses."

Darrell K. Royal (b. 1924)
American college football coach and athletic director

"A manager is best when people barely know that he exists. Not so good when people obey and acclaim him. Worse when they despise him. Fail to honor people, they fail to honor you. But of a good manager, who talks little; when his work is done, his aim fulfilled, they will all say, 'We did this ourselves.'"

Lao-tzu (604–531 B.C.E.)
Chinese philosopher and founder of Taoism

"The fewer rules a coach has, the fewer rules there are for players to break."

John Madden (b. 1936)
former head coach, Oakland Raiders

"There are coaches who spend eighteen hours a day coaching the perfect game and they lose because the ball is oval and they can't control the bounce."

Bud Grant (b. 1927)
American professional football coach

"I've had smarter people around me all my life, but I haven't run into one yet that can outwork me. And if they can't outwork you, then smarts aren't going to do them much good. That's just the way it is. And if you believe that and live by it, you'd be surprised at how much fun you can have."

Woody Hayes (1913–1987)
American college football coach

"No coach ever won a game by what he knows; it's what his players have learned."

Amos Alonzo Stagg (1862–1965)
American college football coach

"This is the first time I've had a kicker who could play with pain. Most of them play with passports."

Larry Lacewell
American college football coach

"My successor is a perfectionist. If he married Raquel Welch, he'd expect her to cook."

Al McGuire (1928–2001)
American college basketball coach and sportscaster
(on Hank Raymonds, his replacement
at Marquette University)

"Managing is like holding a dove in your hand. Squeeze too hard and you kill it; not hard enough and it flies away."

Tommy Lasorda (b. 1927)
American baseball manager

"Some players you pat their butts, some players you kick their butts, some players you leave alone."

Pete Rose (b. 1941)
American baseball player and manager

"You can only really yell at the players you trust."

Bill Parcells (b. 1941)
American football coach

"When I get through managing, I'm going to open up a kindergarten."

Billy Martin (1928–1989)
American baseball player and manager

"Managers must have the discipline not to keep pulling up the flowers to see if their roots are healthy."

Robert Townsend (1920–1998)
American business writer and former president,
Avis-Rent-A-Car, Inc.

"The worst thing about managing is the day you realize you want to win more than the players do."

Gene Mauch (b. 1925)
American baseball manager

"As a manager, you always have a gun to your head. It's a question of whether there is a bullet in the barrel."

Kevin Keegan (b. 1951)
British soccer player and manager

"Sometimes it's frightening when you see a 19-year-old kid running down the floor with your paycheck in his mouth."

Bob Zufplatz
American college basketball coach

"As I grow older, I pay less attention to what men say, I just watch what they do."

Andrew Carnegie (1835–1919)
American industrialist and philanthropist

"If you aren't fired with enthusiasm, you will be fired with enthusiasm."

Vince Lombardi (1913–1970)
American professional football coach

"A successful coach is one who is still coaching."

Ben Schwartzwalder (1909–1993)
American football coach

"It's a pity to shoot the pianist when the piano is out of tune."

René Coty (1882–1962)
French statesman

"There's only two kinds of coaches: them that's been fired and them that's about to be fired."

Bum Phillips (b. 1923)
American professional football coach, formerly with the Houston Oilers and New Orleans Saints

"My gum company made a $40 million profit last year, and I can't get the financial writers to say a word about it. But I fire a manager and everybody shows up."

Philip K. Wrigley (1894–1977)
American executive and owner, Chicago Cubs professional baseball club

"When a coach is hired, he's fired. The date just hasn't been filled in yet."

C.W. Newton
American college basketball coach

"I'm the only coach in history to go straight from the White House to the outhouse."

Pepper Rodgers (b. 1931)
American college football coach
(on being fired as Georgia Tech coach the day after he had lunch with President Jimmy Carter)

"When I first became a manager, I asked Chuck [Tanner] for advice. He told me, 'Always rent.'"

Tony LaRussa (b. 1944)
American professional baseball manager

"There are close to 11 million unemployed and half of them are New York Yankee managers."

Johnny Carson (b. 1925)
American comedian

"I can think of three managers who weren't fired: John McGraw of the Giants, who was sick and resigned; Miller Huggins of the Yankees, who died on the job; and Connie Mack of the Athletics, who owned the club."

Red Smith (1905–1982)
American sportswriter

"I left because of illness and fatigue. The fans were sick and tired of me."

John Ralston (b. 1927)
American professional football coach
(explaining his 1976 ouster as head coach of the Denver Broncos)

"When I got into the coaching business, I knew I was getting into a high-risk, high-profile profession, so I adopted a philosophy I have never wavered from. Yesterday is a canceled check; today is cash on the line; tomorrow is a promissory note."

Hank Stram (b. 1924)
American professional football coach

"If my manager calls, get his name."

Anonymous

"God give me the serenity to accept things which cannot be changed; Give me courage to change things which must be changed; and the wisdom to distinguish one from the other."

attributed to Reinhold Niebuhr (1892–1971)
American theologian
(used as a prayer by Alcoholics Anonymous since 1940)

"If I have seen further it is by standing on the shoulders of giants."

Sir Isaac Newton (1642–1727)
English mathematician and physicist

"Don't be irreplaceable. If you can't be replaced, you can't be promoted."

Anonymous

"I've been here so long that when I got here, the Dead Sea wasn't even sick."

Wimp Sanderson (b. 1937)
American college basketball coach
(on his 32 years as basketball coach at the University of Alabama; he retired the following year following allegations of punching his secretary)

"If he works for you, you work for him."

Japanese proverb

"The best executive is the one who has the sense enough to pick good men to do what he wants done, and self-restraint enough to keep from meddling with them while they do it."

Theodore Roosevelt (1858–1919)
26th president of the United States (1901–1909)

"If you're the boss and your people fight you openly when they think you're wrong, that's healthy. If your people fight each other openly in your presence for what they believe in, that's healthy. But keep all conflict eyeball to eyeball."

Robert Townsend (1920–1998)
American business writer and former president, Avis-Rent-A-Car, Inc.

"To avoid criticism, do nothing, say nothing, be nothing."

Elbert Hubbard (1856–1915)
American writer

"Good management consists in showing average people how to do the work of superior people."

John D. Rockefeller, Jr. (1874–1960)
American oil magnate and philanthropist

"No 'average' man or woman can be a successful manager. Average is a number. A number has:

No hands to reach out to help;

No heart to beat faster at the success of someone you have helped;

No soul to suffer a bit when one of your people suffers.

An average person lacks the disciplined mind to be tough and the self-confident strength to be gentle."

William A. Marsteller (b. 1914)
American advertising agency executive

"In my first game as head coach I discovered there wasn't any chalk for my pregame discussion. I had to use my ulcer pills to write on the board."

Len Jardine (1937–1990)
American college football coach

"Coaching is giving your players a good design and gettin 'em to play hard."

Bill Parcells (b. 1941)
American football coach

"If you make every game a life-and-death proposition, you're going to have problems. For one thing, you'll be dead a lot."

Dean Smith (b. 1931)
American college basketball coach

"Lots of folks confuse bad management with destiny."

Frank McKinney "Kin" Hubbard (1868–1930)
American humorist

"Don't try to fix the students, fix ourselves first. The good teacher makes the poor student good and the good student superior. When our students fail, we, as teachers, too, have failed."

Marva Collins (b. 1936)
American educator

"No manager ever won no ballgames."

Sparky Anderson (b. 1934)
American baseball manager

"If anything goes bad, I did it. If anything goes semi-good, then we did it. If anything goes real good then you did it. That's all it takes to get people to win football games."

Paul W. "Bear" Bryant (1913–1983)
American college football coach

"When I was duck hunting with Bear Bryant, he shot at one but it kept flying. 'John,' he said, 'there flies a dead duck.' That's confidence."

John McKay (b. 1923)
American college and professional football coach

"When you're right you take the bows, and when you're wrong you make the apologies."

Benjamin Ward (1926–2002)
former police commissioner, New York City

"No, but you can see it from here."

Lou Holtz (b. 1937)
American college football coach
(at a University of Arkansas news conference when asked if Fayetteville was the end of the world)

"I don't think we'll be going back to Alaska. I've seen it. I believe it. I think I'll let it go at that."

Tex Winter (b. 1922)
American college basketball coach
(after his Washington Huskies basketball team played a game in Fairbanks and the temperature fell to 50 below zero)

"The three toughest jobs in the world are president of the United States, mayor of New York, and head football coach at Notre Dame."

Beano Cook (b. 1931)
American sportscaster

"A frightened captain makes a frightened crew."

Lister Sinclair (b. 1921)
Canadian author

"In calm water every ship has a good captain."

Swedish proverb

"My special trouble is that I'm now head-coaching one of the teams I'd want to play."

Steve Sloan (b. 1944)
American football coach and athletic director

"I don't mind starting a season with unknowns. I just don't like finishing a season with a bunch of them."

Lou Holtz (b. 1937)
American football coach

"If you let other people do it for you, they will do it to you."

Robert Anthony (b. 1931)
American attorney and educator

"You have to perform at a consistently higher level than others. That's the mark of a true professional. Professionalism has nothing to do with getting paid for your services."

Joe Paterno (b. 1926)
American college football coach

"Power is the ultimate aphrodisiac."

Henry A. Kissinger (b. 1923)
American educator and U.S. Secretary of State

"How can I intimidate batters if I look like a goddamn ***golf pro***?"

Al Hrabosky (b. 1949)
American professional baseball player
(on being ordered to shave)

"I love long hair and beards and mustaches. Yes, sir. If you want to look like you want to look, dress like you want to dress, act like you want to act, play like you want to play, shoot like you want to shoot, do your own thing, I say, 'Great!' But you're sure as hell not coming to Indiana to play basketball. At Indiana, we're going to do my thing."

Bobby Knight (b. 1940)
American college basketball coach

Chapter 5

FANS

"If you really want to advise me, do it on Saturday afternoon between 1 and 4 o'clock. And you've got 25 seconds to do it, between plays. Not on Monday. I know the right thing to do on Monday."

Alex Agase (b. 1922)
American college football coach

"There are the three things the average man thinks he can do better than anybody else: Build a fire, run a hotel, and manage a baseball team."

Rocky Bridges (b. 1927)
American baseball player and manager

"Three years ago at dusk on a spring evening, when the sky was a robin's-egg blue and the wind as soft as a day-old chick, I was sitting on the verandah of my farm home in eastern Iowa when a voice very clearly said to me, 'If you build it, he will come.'"

W. P. Kinsella (b. 1935)
Canadian author
(reference to banished Chicago White Sox player Shoeless Joe Jackson [1889–1951] and story line for the award-winning motion picture Field of Dreams*)*

"Baseball is like church. Many attend. Few understand."

Leo Durocher (1905–1991)
American baseball manager

"I find baseball fascinating. It strikes me as a native American ballet—a totally different dance form. Nearly every move in baseball—the wind-up, the pitch, the motion of the infielders—is different from other games. Next to a triple play, baseball's double play is the most exciting and graceful thing in sports."

Alistair Cooke (1908–2004)
English-born essayist and journalist

"Baseball is a dull game only for those with dull minds."

Walter "Red" Smith (1906–1982)
American sportswriter

"Two events are supremely beautiful: the strikeout and the home run. Each is a difficult and unlikely thing flawlessly achieved before your eyes."

William Saroyan (1908–1981)
American playwright and novelist

"I'm working on a new pitch. It's called a strike."

Jim Kern (b. 1949)
American professional baseball player

"The triple is the most exciting play of the game. A triple is like meeting a woman who excites you, spending the evening talking, then taking her home. It drags on and on. You're never sure how it's going to turn out."

George Foster (b. 1949)
American professional baseball player

"Willie Mays and his glove: where triples go to die."

Fresco Thompson (1902–1968)
Los Angeles Dodgers executive

"Scholars concede but cannot explain the amazing chemistry of Cubs fans' loyalty. But their unique steadfastness through thin and thin has something to do with the team's Franciscan simplicity."

George F. Will (b. 1941)
American news commentator and author

"Since 1946, the Cubs have had two problems: They put too few runs on the scoreboard and the other guys put too many. So what is the new management improving? The scoreboard."

George F. Will (b. 1941)
American news commentator and author

"All literary men are Red Sox fans—to be a Yankee fan in a literate society is to endanger your life."

John Cheever (1912–1982)
American writer

"Hating the Yankees is as American as pizza pie, unwed mothers, and cheating on your income tax."

Mike Royko (1932–1997)
American sportswriter

"Whenever a player hits the ball out of the park I have a sense of elation. I feel as if I had done it. To me, every wall or fence is palpably an inhibition. Beyond the bleacher roof lies Italy."

Heywood Hale Broun (1888–1955)
American journalist

"There's sort of a universal wish among all of us to be the great American sports hero. Thurber once said that 95 percent of the male population puts themselves to sleep striking out the lineup of the New York Yankees. It's the great daydream, an idea that you never quite give up. Always, somewhere in the back of your mind, you believe that Casey Stengel will give you a call."

George Plimpton (1927–2003)
American author and editor

"One of the greatest diseases is to be nobody to anybody."

Mother Teresa (1910–1997)
Roman Catholic nun and humanitarian

"A celebrity is a person who works hard all his life to become well known, then wears dark glasses to avoid being recognized."

Fred Allen (1894–1956)
American comedian

"Kids should practice autographing baseballs. This is a skill that's often overlooked in Little League."

Frank Edwin "Tug" McGraw (1944–2004)
American professional baseball player

"Fans don't boo nobodies."

Reggie Jackson (b. 1946)
American professional baseball player

"All the extraordinary men I have ever known were chiefly extraordinary in their own estimation."

Woodrow Wilson (1856–1924)
28th president of the United States (1913–1921)

"In America, it is sport that is the opiate of the masses."

Russell Baker (b. 1925)
American journalist

"Professional sports add something to the spirit and vitality of a city. They are a reflection of the city's image of itself. I don't simply believe that; I know it. A winning team can bring a city together, and even a losing team can provide a bond of common misery."

Bill Veeck (1914–1986)
American baseball team owner

"I went to a boxing match the other night and a hockey game broke out."

Rodney Dangerfield (b. 1921–2004)
American actor and comedian

"Hockey's the only place where a guy can go nowadays and watch two white guys fight."

Frank Deford (b. 1938)
American sportswriter

"How would you like a job where, if you made a mistake, a big red light goes on and 18,000 people boo?"

Jacques Plante (1929–1986)
Canadian-born National Hockey League goalie

"A race track is a place where windows clean people."

Danny Thomas (1914–1991)
American actor

"An atheist is a guy who watches a Notre Dame-SMU football game and doesn't care who wins."

Dwight D. Eisenhower (1890–1969)
34th president of the United States (1953–1961)

"A spectator is a person who sits forty rows up in the stands and wonders why a seventeen-year-old kid can't hit another seventeen- year-old kid with a ball from forty yards away . . . and then he goes out to the parking lot and can't find his car."

Chuck Mills (b. 1928)
American college football coach

"The guy with the biggest stomach will be the first to take off his shirt at a baseball game."

Glenn Dickey
American sportswriter

"I put my suitcase down, looked up at the Sears Tower and said, 'Chicago, I'm going to conquer you.' When I looked down, my suitcase was gone."

James "Quick" Tillis (b. 1957)
American heavyweight boxer
(on the welcome he received when he moved to the Windy City from his native Oklahoma)

"Philadelphia fans would boo a funeral."

Bo Belinsky (1936–2001)
American professional baseball player

"They read their sports pages, know their statistics, and either root like hell or boo our butts off. I love it. Give me vocal fans—pro or con—over the tourist types who show up in Houston or Montreal and just sit there."

Mike Schmidt (b. 1949)
American professional baseball player

"I have discovered, in 20 years of moving around a ballpark, that the knowledge of the game is usually in inverse proportion to the price of the seats."

Bill Veeck (1914–1986)
American baseball team owner

"Knowing all about baseball is just about as profitable as being a good whittler."

Frank McKinley "Kin" Hubbard (1868–1930)
American humorist

"We formed a booster club in Utah, but by the end of the season it had turned into a terrorist group."

Frank Layden (b. 1931)
American professional basketball coach

"Every crowd has a silver lining."

Phineas Taylor "P.T." Barnum (1910–1891)
American circus owner and showman

"I'd rather have them out at the park booing than at home kicking the television set or complaining that the movie was lousy."

Earl Weaver (b. 1930)
American baseball manager
(on fans)

"Price is what you pay. Value is what you get."

Warren Buffett (b. 1930)
American investor

"If the people don't want to come out to the park, nobody's going to stop 'em."

Yogi Berra (b. 1925)
American baseball player and manager

"'I would like to take the great DiMaggio fishing,' the old man said. 'They say his father was a fisherman. Maybe he was as poor as we are and would understand.'"

Ernest Hemingway (1899–1961)
American author
(from The Old Man and the Sea*)*

"Some day, I would like to go up in the stands and boo some fans."

Bo Belinsky (1936–2001)
American professional baseball player

"People are frustrated these days. The times are vexing, the inflation ever escalating, the problems of daily living overwhelming. Sports, for the masses, are a prime means of escape from those problems. It is at the playing arena that people can let their emotions loose, or at least so they think."

Howard Cosell (1920–1995)
American sportscaster and author

"If they worked as hard at their jobs as I do at mine, this country wouldn't have the inflation problem it has now."

Mike Marshall (b. 1960)
American professional baseball player
(on being booed by Minnesota Twins fans)

"One should never wear one's best trousers to go out and battle for freedom and truth."

Henrik Ibsen (1828–1906)
Norwegian poet and dramatist

"I am reminded of Bill Bingham's observation of a Saturday afternoon at Harvard's Memorial Stadium—22 boys on the field badly in need of rest, and 40,000 people in the stands badly in need of exercise."

Robert F. Kennedy (1925–1968)
U.S. Attorney General and Senator

"As a nation we are dedicated to keeping physically fit—and parking as close to the stadium as possible."

Bill Vaughan (1915–1977)
American sportswriter

"The sad fact is that it looks more and more as if our national sport is not playing at all—but watching."

John F. Kennedy (1917–1963)
35th president of the United States (1961–1963)
(on whether baseball or football is America's national pasttime)

"The three most phony things in football are artificial turf, domed stadiums, and the Wave."

John Madden (b. 1936)
American football coach and television sports analyst

"How can you hit inside a dome when you grew up listening to your mother tell you not to play ball inside the house?"

Joe Garagiola (b. 1926)
American baseball player and sportscaster

MOST DISLIKED SPORTS

Although baseball has long advertised itself as America's pasttime, regularly conducted popularity polls consistently show that baseball's position at the top of the sports popularity list has long been supplanted by football. In fact, a recent poll reported *football* (that Europeans—who consider the term football to be restricted to soccer—and often refer to the sport as *gridiron*) is currently more than twice as popular as national pasttime. Basketball is typically listed in a virtual tie with baseball in second place.

But what would a poll conducted to identify America's most loathed sports include? A recent telephone survey of 1,000 respondents conducted by the Atlanta-based Sports Marketing Group came up with the following list:

1. Dog Fighting: hated or disliked a lot by 81 percent of the public
2. Pro Wrestling: farcial and more than a little trashy, disliked by more than half the nation.
3. Bullfighting: Americans don't get it, never see it, and apparently don't want it.
4. Professional boxing: violent sport loathed by 31 percent of the public—in particular, by women.

These are followed, in order of dislike, by the PGA Tour (30 percent); the PGA Seniors' Champions Tour (30 percent), the LPGA Tour (29 percent), NASCAR (28 percent), Major League Soccer (28 percent), and the ATP men's tennis tour (27 percent). Although golf sometimes suffers from a snooty and sexist country club image that may not fit reality, its popularity among African-Americans soared during the past decade in the age of Tiger Woods.

Sports Marketing Group survey data reported in Steve Wilstein, "Some Sports Draw Jeers," Mobile Register, *September 9, 2003, p. C2.*

Chapter 6

Enforcers: Umpires, Referees, and Judges

"The best thing is to play;
The second best is to coach;
And the third best is to officiate the sport you love."

Dr. Henry Nichols
American basketball referee

"We're supposed to be perfect our first day on the job, and then show constant improvement."

Ed Vargo (b. 1923)
American baseball umpire

American major league baseball umpire, *You've Got to Have Balls to Make It in This League*

Pam Postema (b. 1954)
(book title detailing her unsuccessful effort to become the first female umpire in Major League Baseball)

"The only way to succeed is to make people hate you."

Josef von Sternberg (1894–1969)
American film director

"Ideally, the umpire should combine the integrity of a Supreme Court justice, the physical agility of an acrobat, the endurance of Job, and the imperturbability of Buddha."

Time

"I don't know the key to success, but the key to failure is trying to please everybody."

Bill Cosby (b. 1937)
American actor and comedian

"Umpires should be natural Republicans—dead to human feelings."

George F. Will (b. 1941)
American news commentator and author

"Officials are the only guys who can rob you and then get a police escort out of the stadium."

Ron Bolton (b. 1950)
American professional football player

"There is no such thing as a corrupt umpire . . . and there never will be!"

Warren Giles (1896–1979)
National League president

"Boys, I'm one of those umpires that misses 'em every once in a while. So if it's close, you'd better hit it."

Cal P. Hubbard (1900–1977)
American baseball umpire

"I couldn't see well enough to play when I was a boy, so they gave me a special job—they made me the umpire."

Harry S Truman (1884–1972)
33rd president of the United States (1945–1953)

"Dark charged out on the field and I was shocked at the language he used. He suggested there had not been a marriage in my family for three generations."

Bill Valentine
American baseball umpire
(explaining why he ejected Cleveland Indians manager
Alvin Dark [b. 1922] from a game)

"I occasionally get birthday cards from fans. But it's often the same message: They hope it's my last."

Al Foreman (1903–1954)
American baseball umpire

"The first and great commandment is 'Don't let them scare you'."

Elmer Davis (1890–1958)
American radio broadcaster and news commentator

"It's a strange business, all jeers and no cheers."

Tom Gorman (1919–1986)
American baseball umpire

"Officiating is the only occupation in the world where the highest accolade is silence."

Earl Strom (1927–1994)
American professional basketball referee

"The worst-tempered people I've ever met were the people who knew they were wrong."

Wilson Mizner (1876–1933)
American author

"The way to test the durability of a Timex watch would be to strap it to his tongue."

Marty Springstead (b. 1937)
American baseball umpire (on former Baltimore Orioles manager Earl Weaver)

"Hindsight is an exact science."

Guy Bellamy (b. 1935)
American journalist

"If thou art a master, be sometimes blind; if a servant, sometimes deaf."

Thomas Fuller (1608–1661)
English clergyman and author

"See everything, overlook a great deal, correct a little."

Pope John XXIII (1881–1963)

"In all my years as an umpire, I've never had a person come up to me and say, 'Are you Nestor Chylak, the umpire?'"

Nestor Chylak (1922–1982)
American baseball umpire

"Too bad all the people who know how to make the correct calls are busy cutting hair and driving taxis."

Anonymous

"Cab drivers are proof that practice doesn't make perfect."

John Winokur
British author

Chapter 7

Sportscasters, Reporters, and the Media

"There are superb books about golf, very good books about baseball, not many good books about football, and very few good books about basketball. There are no books about beach balls."

George Plimpton (1927–2003)
American author and editor
(on the inverse correlation between the size of a ball and the quality of books written about the sport in which the ball is used)

"Many an All-American has been made by a long run, a weak defense, and a poet in the press box."

Robert Zuppke (1879–1957)
American college football coach

"Outlined against a blue-grey October sky, the four Horsemen rode again. In dramatic lore they are known as Famine, Pestilence, Destruction, and Death. Their real names are Stuhldreher, Miller, Crowley, and Layden."

Grantland Rice (1880–1954)
American sportswriter
(describing the 1924 Notre Dame backfield)

"I always turn to the sports pages first, which record people's accomplishments. The front page has nothing but man's failures."

Earl Warren (1891–1974)
Chief Justice of the U.S. Supreme Court (1953–1969)

"I'd rather be on the sports page than on the front page."

Gerald R. Ford (b. 1913)
38th president of the United States (1974–1977)

"Baseball is the best sport for a writer to cover, because it's daily. It's ongoing. You have to fill the need, write the daily soap opera."

Peter Gammons (b. 1945)
American sportswriter

"Baseball is the most intellectual game because most of the action goes on in your head."

Henry A. Kissinger (b. 1923)
American educator and U.S. Secretary of State

"Look at it this way: If most sportswriters were any good at what they did, they would be novelists instead of sportswriters."

George O'Leary (b. 1946)
American college football coach
(responding to the selection by sportswriters of the University of Colorado as America's No. 1 football team for 1990 rather than his undefeated Georgia Tech team)

"Media, the plural of mediocrity."

Jimmy Breslin (b. 1930)
American journalist

"To get a job you've either got to be pretty or be a big star or both. Heck, any guy who can string two sentences together and look good at the same time can be a sportscaster."

Jim Bouton (b. 1939)
American baseball player and author

"A color commentator is a guy who's paid to talk when everyone goes to the bathroom."

Bill Curry (b. 1942)
American college football coach and sportscaster

"Whoever writes for any reason other than for money is a blockhead."

Samuel Johnson (1709–1784)
English lexicographer and writer

"The tools I need for my work are paper, tobacco, food, and a little whiskey."

William Faulkner (1897–1962)
American novelist

"Sports writing is the most pleasant way of making a living that man has yet devised."

Walter "Red" Smith (1905–1982)
American sportswriter

"I like the job I have now, but, if I had my life to live over again, I'd like to have ended up as a sportswriter."

Richard M. Nixon (1913–94)
37th president of the United States (1969–1974)

"If all sports prognosticators were laid end to end they would not reach a conclusion."

Anonymous

"If all sports prognosticators were laid end to end, they would point in all directions."

Anonymous

"And we're going to win Sunday—I'll guarantee it."

Joe Namath (b. 1943)
American professional football player
(correctly predicting a victory for his New York Jets in the 1969 Super Bowl, even though the Baltimore Colts were prohibitive favorites)

"Arrogant, pompous, obnoxious, vain, cruel, persecuting, distasteful, verbose, a show-off. I have been called all of these. Of course, I am."

Howard Cosell (1920–1995)
American sportscaster and author

"Even the lion has to defend himself against flies."

German proverb

"Ronald Reagan has held the two most demeaning jobs in the country: president of the United States and radio broadcaster of the Chicago Cubs."

George F. Will (b. 1941)
American news commentator and author

"The toughest job for a coach today is handling the press after a game."

Hector Blake (1912–1995)
Canadian professional hockey coach

"Most women in this business don't cover games. Ninety percent of us don't. The standard idea of a woman sportswriter's story is doing Steve Garvey's wife or writing a feature about Nancy Lopez. The men on the beat are always aware of that. This is why locker-room access is the heart of it all. Access is the key to covering games, and you aren't a sportswriter—you haven't paid your dues—unless you cover games."

Betty Cuniberti
American sportswriter

"No one should have to dance backward all their lives."

Jill Ruckelshaus (b. 1937)
U.S. Commission on Civil Rights officer

"The players and the reporters are bound together inextricably, like partners in a dance."

Bill Bradley (b. 1943)
American professional basketball player
and former U.S. Senator

"A sportswriter is entombed in a prolonged boyhood."

Jimmy Cannon (1909–1973)
American sportswriter

"If I ever needed a brain transplant, I'd choose a sportswriter because I'd want a brain that had never been used."

Norm Van Brocklin (1926–1983)
American professional football player

"The Lord taught me to love everybody. But the last ones the Lord taught me to love were the sportswriters."

Alvin Dark (b. 1922)
American baseball player and manager

"In dealing with the press, do yourself a favor: stick with one of three responses: I know and I can tell you; I know and I can't tell you; and I don't know."

Dan Rather (b. 1931)
American newscaster

"Mr. Hume:

I've read your review of my daughter Margaret's concert last night and I've come to the conclusion that you're an eight-ulcer man on four-ulcer pay. And after reading such poppycock, it's obvious that you're off the beam and that at least four of your ulcers are working overtime. I hope to meet you and when I do, you're going to need a new nose, plenty of beefsteak for black eyes, and perhaps a jockstrap below."

Harry S Truman (1884–1972)
33rd president of the United States (1945–1953)
(response to Washinqton Post *music critic*
Paul Hume's negative review of
his daughter Margaret's singing)

"Congress shall make no law abridging the freedom of speech or of the press."

Amendment I of the United States Constitution

"All I know is what I see in the papers."

Will Rogers (1879–1935)
American actor and humorist

"Four hostile newspapers are more to be feared than a thousand bayonets."

Napoleon Bonaparte (1769–1821)
French emperor (1804–1815)

"I never played the game."

Howard Cosell (1920–1995)
American sportscaster and author

"Nothing is real unless it happens on television."

Daniel J. Boorstin (1914–2004)
American historian and Librarian of Congress

"People forget that TV is not free. The consumer eventually pays for those enormous rights fees, whether he's paying Russia for the Olympics or the NFL for *Monday Night Football.* The costs are passed along through almost every product advertised on television. One estimate is that several hundred dollars of the cost of a new car represent TV advertising; it's a nickel on every tube of toothpaste; and so on. So when we talk about the price of TV sports going up, it's significant because it affects everything else."

David A. Klatell
American educator

"Television is an invention that permits you to be entertained in your living room by people you wouldn't have in your home."

David Frost (b. 1939)
English entertainer

"[Watching television] is now the dominant leisure of American consumers, consuming 40 percent of the average person's free time as a primary activity."

Todd Gitlin (b. 1942)
American author and professor of journalism, culture, and sociology at Columbia University

"The greed in college athletics has taken over. The loyalties between institutions and conferences are not there anymore. Television has taken over."

Joe Gottfried (b. 1940)
American college athletic director

"TV exposure is so important to our program and so important to this university that we will schedule ourselves to fit the medium. I'll play at midnight, if that's what TV wants."

Paul W. "Bear" Bryant (1913–1983)
American college football coach

"Journalism is a kind of profession, or craft, or racket, for people who never wanted to grow up and go out into the real world. If you're a good journalist, what you do is live a lot of things vicariously and report them for other people who want to live vicariously."

Harry Reasoner (1923–1991)
American television news reporter

"A sportswriter is an expert who will explain in tomorrow's column why the things he predicted yesterday didn't happen today."

Anonymous

"Well-meaning people often ask sportswriters, even middle-aged sportswriters, what they are going to do when they grow up."

Robert Lipsyte (b. 1938)
American sportswriter

Chapter 8

OWNERS, AGENTS, AND ATTORNEYS

"I always wanted to be a player, but I never had the talent to make the big leagues. So I did the next best thing: I bought a team."

Charles O. Finley (1918–1997)
American baseball team owner

"I want this team to win. I'm obsessed with winning, with discipline, with achieving. That's what this country's all about."

George Steinbrenner (b. 1930)
American executive and owner, New York Yankees professional baseball club

"I don't want any yes-men around me. I want everyone to tell me the truth—even though it costs him his job."

Samuel Goldwyn (1882–1974)
American motion picture producer

"Firing people is unpleasant, but it really has to be done occasionally. Purging the bad performers is as good a tonic for the organization as giving sizable rewards to the star performers."

Robert Townsend (1920–1998)
American business writer and former president, Avis-Rent-A-Car, Inc.

"It isn't the people you fire who will make your life miserable; it's the people you don't fire."

Harvey Mackay (b. 1933)
American executive and business writer

"First-rate people hire first-rate people; second-rate people hire third-rate people."

Leo Rosten (1908–1997)
American writer

"It is much more secure to be feared than to be loved."

Niccolo Machiavelli (1469–1527)
Italian political philosopher

"Though familiarity may not breed contempt, it takes the edge off admiration."

William Hazlitt (1778–1830)
English essayist and critic

"Fifteen or twenty years ago, I was wandering around Arkansas, and Bill Clinton was, too. Who would have ever thought that one would go on to power, prestige, and fame . . . and the other would end up president of the United States?"

Jerry Jones (b. 1942)
owner, Dallas Cowboys football team

"The graveyards are full of indispensable men."

Charles de Gaulle (1890–1970)
French general and president of the Fifth Republic

"It's sort of like somebody hitting you on the head with a 2-by- 4. After a while, you get used to it. But you sure do notice when it stops."

Fay Vincent (b. 1938)
Major League Baseball Commissioner
(after collective bargaining agreement ended
1990 lockout and weeks of negotiations)

"Soldiers win battles and generals get the credit."

Napoleon Bonaparte (1769–1821)
Emperor of France (1804–1815)

"Never follow the crowd."

Bernard Baruch (1870–1965)
American financier and statesman

"Unless you enter the tiger's den you cannot take the cubs."

Japanese proverb

"You miss 100 percent of the shots you never take."

Wayne Gretzky (b. 1961)
Canadian-born professional hockey star

"People do not understand the importance of failure in achievement. We have to be willing to risk failure. There is no way we can realize our full potential unless we have failed so many times that eventually we learn the lesson necessary for us to go on to our great achievements."

Brian Tracy
American author

"I gave him an unlimited budget—and he exceeded it."

Edward Bennett Williams (1920–1988)
American lawyer and former Washington Redskins football club owner
(on his former head coach George Allen [1918–1990])

"The next time you see a headline about a television network spending a billion dollars for the rights to televise some sports event, think about it this way: If you spent $100,000 every day of the week, it would take you more than 27 years to spend a billion dollars."

David L. Kurtz (b. 1941)
American educator and business writer

"Baseball is too much of a sport to be a business and too much of a business to be a sport."

Philip K. Wrigley (1894–1977)
American executive and owner, Chicago Cubs professional baseball club

"When the Supreme Court says baseball isn't run like a business, everybody jumps up and down with joy. When I say the same thing, everybody throws pointed objects at me."

Bill Veeck (1914–1986)
American baseball team owner

"Boxing is a great sport and a dirty business."

Ken Norton (b. 1944)
World heavyweight boxing champion, 1978

"Coaching has changed. Twenty years ago, the coach never left the campus. Now I balance the budget, market the product, do promotions, handle personnel, sell the program, recruit, and coach. Like it or not, it's a different type of business now."

Jackie Sherrill (b. 1943)
American college football coach

"I ask a player, 'Are you happy with this contract?' He'll say, yes he is. 'Fine,' I tell him, 'I'm happy, too. We're both happy. But I have one provision before we sign this contract. There will not be any renegotiation, because I want you to be aware that if you get hurt, we pay the full contract and if you have a bad year, we're still obligated to pay. Remember, you have security and peace of mind for two to three years. You have everything. Don't ever ask to renegotiate a term contract with me. Remember, you're the one who asked for it in the first place.'"

Arnold "Red" Auerbach (b. 1917)
former basketball coach and general manager of the NBA's Boston Celtics

"I had a better year than he did."

Babe Ruth (1895–1948)
American professional baseball player
(on being told that President Hoover made less than the $80,000 he was demanding in 1930.)

"We just received a message from Saddam Hussein. The good news is that he's willing to have his nuclear, biological, and chemical weapons counted. The bad news is, he wants Arthur Anderson to do it."

George W. Bush (b. 1946)
43rd president of the United States (2001–)

"We run our club like a pawn shop; we buy, we trade, we sell."

Charles O. Finley (1918–1997)
American baseball team owner

"I once loved this game. But after being traded four times, I realize that it's nothing but a business. I treat my horses better than the owners treat us."

Dick Allen (b. 1942)
American professional baseball player

"After 12 years in the major leagues I do not feel that I am a piece of property to be bought and sold irrespective of my wishes. I believe that any system that produces that result violates my basic rights as a citizen and is inconsistent with the laws of the United States and several states."

Curt Flood (1938–1997)
American professional baseball player
(protesting his 1969 trade from the St. Louis Cardinals to the Philadelphia Phillies; shortly afterward, Flood filed an antitrust lawsuit against Organized Baseball)

"The *lack* of money is the root of all evil."

George Bernard Shaw (1856–1950)
British author and social reformer

"What is a cynic? A man who knows the price of everything and the value of nothing."

Oscar Wilde (1854–1900)
Irish poet, playwright and novelist

"Only a fool holds out for the top dollar."

Joseph P. Kennedy (1888–1969)
American businessman and diplomat

"We're overpaying him, but he's worth it."

Samuel Goldwyn (1882–1974)
American motion picture producer

"It isn't really the stars that are expensive. It's the high cost of mediocrity."

Bill Veeck (1914–1986)
American baseball team owner

"That's like Al Capone speaking out for gun control."

William F. "Blackie" Sherrod (b. 1920)
American sportswriter
(on Atlanta Braves owner Ted Turner's complaint that baseball salaries are too high)

"He that speaks ill of the mare will buy her."

Benjamin Franklin (1706–1790)
American statesman and philosopher

"I don't mind paying a player, but I don't want to pay for his funeral."

Pat Gillick (b. 1937)
American baseball club executive
(on 39-year-old Rico Carty's demand for a three-year contract)

"When two teams are interested, you negotiate; when only one team is interested, you beg."

Mark Schlereth (b. 1966)
Denver Broncos professional football player

"If you want a kitten, start out by asking for a pony."

Anonymous

"A complete ballplayer today is one who can hit, field, run, throw, and pick the right agent."

Bob Lurie (b. 1924)
American baseball team owner

"Throughout the history of commercial life nobody has ever quite liked the commission man. His function is too vague, his presence always seems one too many, his profit looks too easy, and even when you admit that he has a necessary function, you feel that this function is as it were a personification of something that in an ethical society would not need to exist. If people could deal with one another honestly, they would not need agents."

Raymond Chandler (1888–1958)
American author

"I'm not an agent. I'm an engineer of careers."

Mark H. McCormack (1930–2003)
founder and former chairman, IMG Sports Management

"Lawyers are like beavers. They get in the mainstream and dam it up."

John Naisbitt (b. 1929)
American business writer and social researcher

"The minute you read something that you can't understand, you can almost be sure it was drawn up by a lawyer."

Will Rogers (1879–1935)
American actor and humorist

"A verbal contract isn't worth the paper it's written on."

Samuel Goldwyn (1882–1974)
American motion picture producer

"I would like to apologize to the bird species for connecting these two."

Mike Gottfried (b. 1940)
American college football coach and sports analyst
(on his referring to sports agents as "vultures")

"I think an agent should get paid by the hour. I don't believe anyone should own a percentage of anyone else. That's one of the reasons we fought the Civil War."

Al McGuire (1928–2001)
American college basketball coach and sportscaster

"There are three reasons why sports agents are being used more and more as subjects in scientific experiments. First, every year there are more and more of them. Second, lab assistants don't get attached to them. And, third, there are some things that rats just won't do."

Anonymous

Part 3

The Art and Science of Sports Marketing and Management

Chapter 9

Strategies for Achieving Sports Objectives

"The idea in this game isn't to win popularity polls or to be a good guy to everyone. The name of the game is *win*."

Billy Martin (1928–1989)
American baseball player and manager

"Business is a combination of war and sport."

Andre Maurois (1885–1967)
French writer

"I don't like them fellas who drive in two runs and let in three."

Casey Stengel (1890–1975)
American baseball manager

"Before you can score you must first have a goal."

Anonymous

"Once you say you're going to settle for second, that's what happens to you in life, I find."

John F. Kennedy (1917–1963)
35th president of the United States (1961–1963)

"My interest is in the future because I am going to spend the rest of my life there."

Charles F. Kettering (1876–1958)
American electrical engineer and inventor

"I've seen the future and it's much like the present, only longer."

Dan Quisenberry (1953–1998)
American professional baseball player

"To finish first you must first finish."

Rick Mears (b. 1951)
American race car driver

"There is no finish line."

Nike Corporation motto

"We've changed our uniforms. We look a lot like the Pittsburgh Steelers. Until the ball is snapped."

Hayden Fry (b. 1929)
American college football coach (after becoming head coach at Iowa University in 1979 when the Hawkeyes had just completed their 18th straight losing season)

"This year we plan to run and shoot. Next season we hope to run and score."

Billy Tubbs (b. 1935)
American college basketball coach

"Ah, but a man's reach should exceed his grasp—or what's a heaven for?"

Robert Browning (1812–1889)
English poet

"Fixing your objective is like identifying the North Star—you sight your compass on it and then use it as the means of getting back on the track when you tend to stray."

Marshall E. Dimock (1903–1991)
American author

"My philosophy of life is that if we make up our mind what we are going to make of our lives, then work hard toward that goal, we never lose—somehow we win out."

Ronald Reagan (1911–2004)
40th president of the United States (1981–1989)

"First we will be best, and then we will be first."

Grant Tinker (b. 1926)
American television executive

"Without some goal and some efforts to reach it, no man can live."

Fyodor Dosteovsky (1821–1881)
Russian author

"If you can dream it, you can do it."

Walt Disney (1901–1966)
American film producer

"Never lose hope in your dreams. For without dreams, life is a broken-winged bird that cannot fly."

Langston Hughes (1902–1967)
American poet

"I think I can. I think I can."

Little Engine That Could

"A dream doesn't become reality through magic; it takes sweat, determination, and hard work."

General Colin Powell (b. 1937)
American military leader and U.S. secretary of state

"Don't be afraid to take a big step. You can't cross a chasm in two small jumps."

David Lloyd George (1863–1945)
British statesman and Prime Minister (1916–1922)

"I dream of big things. I work for the small things."

Kevin Costner (b. 1955)
American actor

"I have studied the enemy all my life. I have read the memoirs of his generals and his leaders. I have even read his philosophers and listened to his music. I have studied in detail the account of every damned one of his battles. I know exactly how he will react under any given set of circumstances. And he hasn't the slightest idea of what I'm going to do. So when the time comes, I'm going to whip the hell out of him."

George S. Patton (1885–1945)
General, U.S. Army

"The race may not be to the swift nor the victory to the strong, but that's how you bet."

Damon Runyon (1884–1946)
American author

"Make no little plans; they have no magic to stir men's blood and probably themselves will not be realized. Make big plans; aim high in hope and work, remembering that a noble, logical diagram once recorded will not die."

Daniel H. Burnham (1846–1912)
American architect

"The enemy advances, we retreat; the enemy camps, we harass; the enemy tires, we attack; the enemy retreats; we pursue."

Mao Tse-tung (1873–1976)
Chinese communist leader of
Peoples Republic of China

"Carry the battle to them. Don't let them bring it to you. Put them on the defensive. And don't ever apologize for anything."

Harry S Truman (1884–1972)
33rd president of the United States (1945–1953)

"All men can see these tactics whereby I conquer, but what none can see is the strategy out of which victory is evolved."

Sun-tsu (c. 400-341 B.C.E.)
Chinese military strategist

"All strategy depends on competition."

Bruce D. Henderson (b. 1915)
American educator and founder of the Boston
Consulting Group

"No plan can prevent a stupid person from doing the wrong thing in the wrong place at the wrong time—but a good plan should keep a concentration from forming."

Charles E. Wilson (1890–1961)
former chairman, General Motors Corp. and U.S. secretary of defense (1953–1957)

"Plans are nothing; planning is everything."

Dwight D. Eisenhower (1890–1969)
34th president of the United States (1953–1961)

"Every accomplishment starts with the decision to try."

Anonymous

"When you are faced with a decision, the best thing is to do the right thing, the next is to do the wrong thing, and the worst thing is to do nothing."

Roger A. Enrico (b. 1943)
former chairman and CEO, PepsiCo

"Victory goes to the player who makes the next-to-last mistake."

Savielly Grigorievitch Tartakower (1837–1956)
International Grand Master of Chess

"Most ball games are lost, not won."

Casey Stengel (1890–1975)
American baseball manager

"Victory often goes to the army that makes the least mistakes, not the most brilliant plans."

Charles de Gaulle (1890–1970)
French general and president of the Fifth Republic

"When in doubt, risk it."

Holbrook Jackson (1874–1948)
English journalist, editor, and author

"If no one ever took risks, Michelangelo would have painted the Sistine floor."

Neil Simon (b. 1927)
American playwright

"In life, as in a football game, the principle to follow is: Hit the line hard."

Theodore Roosevelt (1858–1919)
26th president of the United States (1901–1909)

"The baseline belongs to me."

Ty Cobb (1886–1961)
American professional baseball player

"Cobb is a [jerk]. But he sure can hit. God Almighty, that man can hit."

George Herman "Babe" Ruth (1895–1948)
American professional baseball player

"My name is Ted . . . Williams and I'm the greatest hitter in baseball."

Ted Williams (1918–2002)
American professional baseball player
(words he used to psych himself up before batting)

"Ted Williams was a real hitter. Me, I just got up there and swung for the roof ever' time and waited to see what would happen."

Mickey Mantle (1931–1995)
American professional baseball player

"Four out of five points are won on your opponent's errors. So just hit the ball back over the net."

Bill Talbert (1918–1999)
American professional tennis player

"You can't sit on a lead and run a few plays into the line and just kill the clock. You've got to throw the ball over the goddamn plate and give the other man a chance."

Earl Weaver (b. 1930)
American baseball manager
(on the virtues of baseball over football)

"In football the object is to march into enemy territory and cross his goal. In baseball the object is to go home."

George Carlin (b. 1938)
American comedian

"Golf is not a game of great shots. It's a game of the most misses. The people who win make the smallest mistakes."

Gene Littler (b. 1920)
American professional golfer

"Offense sells tickets but defense wins championships."

Anonymous

"When a thing is done, it's done. Don't look back. Look forward to your next objective."

George C. Marshall (1880–1959)
U.S. Army general and statesman

"Only three things can happen when you put the ball in the air, and two of them are bad."

Duffy Daugherty (1915–1987)
American college football coach

Chapter 10

Leadership

"A team should be an extension of the coach's personality. My teams were arrogant and obnoxious."

Al McGuire (1928–2001)
American college basketball coach and sportscaster

"He's fair. He treats us all the same—like dogs."

Henry Jordan (b. 1955)
American football player
(referring to Green Bay Packers coach Vince Lombardi)

"Treat 'em like dogs, and you'll have dogs' works and dogs' actions. Treat 'em like men, and you'll have men's works."

Harriet Beecher Stowe (1811–1896)
American author

"The pupil who is never required to what he cannot do, never does what he can do."

John Stuart Mill (1806–1873)
English philosopher and economist

"People react to fear, not love. They don't teach that in Sunday school, but it's true."

Richard M. Nixon (1913–1994)
37th president of the United States (1969–1974)

"I never give them hell; I just tell the truth, and they think it's hell."

Harry S Truman (1884–1972)
33rd president of the United States (1945–1953)

"I haven't changed my style in 20 years . . . and that style is to get mad when things go wrong."

Alexander Haig (b. 1924)
former president, United Technologies Corp. and U.S. secretary of state (1981–1982)

"I probably couldn't play for me. I wouldn't like my attitude."

John Thompson (b. 1941)
American college basketball coach

"A mean streak is a very important quality of leadership."

Charles E. Goodell (1926–1987)
American lawyer and U.S. Senator

"If you hit a pony over the nose at the outset of your acquaintance, he may not love you, but he will take a deep interest in your movements ever afterwards."

Rudyard Kipling (1865–1936)
English novelist

"You do not lead by hitting people over the head—that's assault, not leadership."

Dwight D. Eisenhower (1890–1969)
34th president of the United States (1953–1961)

"There's no sense in whipping a tired horse, because he'll quit on you. More horses are whipped out of the money than into it."

Eddie Arcaro (1916–1997)
American jockey

"Successful teams, just like businesses, have an environment where everyone believes in the leader and they perform accordingly."

Carl Banks (b. 1962)
former New York Giants linebacker and current apparel entrepreneur

"To command is to serve, nothing more, and nothing less."

Andre Malraux (1901–1976)
French novelist

Ten Ways To Be A Leader

1. Begin with praise and honest appreciation.
2. Call attention to people's mistakes indirectly.
3. Talk about your own mistakes before criticizing the other person.
4. Ask questions instead of giving direct orders.
5. Let the other person save face.
6. Praise the slightest improvement and praise every improvement.
7. Give the other person a fine reputation to live up to.
8. Use encouragement.
9. Make the fault easy to correct.
10. Make the other person happy about doing the thing you suggest.

Dale Carnegie (1888–1955)
American writer and speaker

"The question 'Who ought to be boss?' is like asking 'Who ought to be tenor in the quartet?' Obviously, the man who can sing tenor."

Henry Ford (1863–1947)
American automobile manufacturer

"Lead, follow, or get out of the way!"

Anonymous

"Any leader worth following gives credit easily where credit is due. He does not take someone's idea, dress it up, and offer it as his own. He offers it as theirs. Otherwise, ideas will soon cease to flow his way. He plays fair with everyone and recognizes the strong points in people as well as the weak ones. He never takes advantage for his own selfish purposes."

Franklin J. Lundling (b. 1906)
American attorney

"We're going to run the organization from the top down. We're controlling player personnel. That's our job. I don't apologize for that. There's this belief that a baseball team starts with the manager first. It doesn't."

Billy Beane (b. 1962)
General Manager, Oakland Athletics professional baseball team

"Sandwich every bit of criticism between two heavy layers of praise."

Mary Kay Ash (1915–2001)
Founder, Mary Kay Cosmetics

"I praise loudly, I blame softly."

Catherine II (The Great) (1729–1796)
Empress of Russia (1762–1796)

"Before you criticize someone, walk a mile in his shoes. Then when you do criticize that person, you'll be a mile away and have his shoes!"

Anonymous

"Managers are people who do things right, and leaders are people who do the right thing."

Warren G. Bennis (b. 1925) and Burt Nanus
American educators and business writers

"If you ain't the lead dog, the scenery never changes."

Buddy Ryan (b. 1934)
American professional football coach
(inscription on a plaque on his desk)

"All mankind is divided into three classes: those who are immovable; those who are movable; and those who move."

Benjamin Franklin (1706–1790)
American statesman and philosopher

"A leader is a dealer in hope."

Napoleon Bonaparte (1769–1821)
Emperor of France (1804–1815)

"The weaker a man in authority . . . the stronger his insistence that all his privileges be acknowledged."

Austin O'Malley (1858–1932)
American writer

"When angry, count four; when very angry, swear."

Mark Twain (1835–1910)
American author

"You cannot manage men into battle. You manage things; you lead people."

Grace Murray Hopper (1906–1992)
Admiral, U.S. Navy

"It is the weak man who urges compromise—never the strong man."

Elbert Hubbard (1856–1915)
American writer

"A man who trims himself to suit everybody will soon whittle himself away."

Charles Schwab (1862–1939)
American industrialist

"There are no bad soldiers under a good general."

Anonymous

"He thinks group, but he always sees individuals."

Bill Bradley (b. 1943)
American professional basketball player and former U.S. Senator (describing his friend, NBA championship coach Phil Jackson's coaching style)

"The first and great commandment is don't let them scare you."

Elmer Davis (1890–1958)
American writer and radio news commentator

"I have an absolute rule. I refuse to make a decision that somebody else can make. The first rule of leadership is to save yourself for the big decision. Don't allow your mind to become cluttered with the trivia. Don't let yourself become the issue."

Richard M. Nixon (1913–1994)
37th president of the United States (1969–1974)

"Many receive advice, few profit by it."

Publilius Syrus (1st century B.C.E.)
Latin writer of mimes

"Being left-handed is a big advantage. No one knows enough about your swing to mess you up with advice."

Bob Charles (b. 1936)
New Zealand professional golfer

"Henry Ford could get anything out of men because he just talked and would tell them stories. He'd never say, 'I want this done.' He'd say, 'I wonder if we can do it.'"

George Brown (1918–1978)
General, U.S. Army

"If you remember the following three words, not only will you be a good leader but the people you lead will, too: Officers eat last. The point is, if you are responsible for your people they will take care of you."

Al Lerner (1933–2002)
former owner, Cleveland Browns
professional football club

"We can't all be heroes because somebody has to sit on the curb and clap as they go by."

Will Rogers (1879–1935)
American actor and humorist

THE MOST IMPORTANT WORDS IN THE ENGLISH LANGUAGE

5 most important words: I am proud of you!

4 most important words: What is your opinion?

3 most important words: If you please.

2 most important words: Thank you.

1 most important word: *You.*

Chapter 11

Motivation

"Fight one more round. When your feet are so tired that you have to shuffle back to the center of the ring, fight one more round. When your arms are so tired that you can hardly lift your hands to come on guard, fight one more round. When your nose is bleeding and your eyes are black and you are so tired that you wish your opponent would crack you one on the jaw and put you to sleep, fight one more round—remembering that the man who always fights one more round is never whipped."

James J. Corbett (1866–1933)
World heavyweight boxing champion, 1892–1897

"Heroism consists of hanging on one minute longer."

Norwegian proverb

"You may not think you're going to make it. You may want to quit. But if you keep your eye on the ball, you can accomplish anything."

Hank Aaron (b. 1934)
American professional baseball player

"Four little words sum up what has lifted most successful individuals above the crowd: *a little bit more.* They did all that was expected of them and a little bit more."

A. Lou Vickery (b. 1941)
American business writer

"In 1975, I was the best tennis player in the whole world. It doesn't matter how long you're there, or if you ever get there again, you got there. Not too many ever get there in anything. It's a damn exclusive club."

Arthur Ashe (1943–1993)
American professional tennis player

"Because it's there."

George H.L. Mallory (1886–1924)
English mountain climber
(explaining why he wanted to climb Mt. Everest)

"Nobody climbs mountains for scientific reasons. Science is used to raise money for the expeditions, but you really climb for the hell of it."

Sir Edmund Hillary (b. 1919)
New Zealand mountain climber and explorer
(with Tensing Norgay [c. 1914–c. 1986],
the first to climb Mt. Everest)

"If you think you can win, you can win. Faith is necessary to victory."

William Hazlitt (1778–1830)
English essayist and critic

"Win one for the Gipper."

attributed to Knute Rockne (1888–1931)
Norwegian-born college football coach
(exhorting his Notre Dame football team before a 1921 game by referring to their All-American teammate, George Gipp, who had died a few months earlier)

"Even youths grow tired and weary,
and young men stumble and fall
but those who hope in the Lord
will renew their strength.
They will soar on wings like eagles;
they will run and not grow weary,
they will walk and not be faint."

Bible. *Isaiah 40:30–31*

"The great pleasure in life is doing what people say you cannot do."

Walter Bagehot (1826–1877)
English economist and journalist

"Do something worth remembering."

Elvis Presley (1935–1977)
American singer

"All I want out of life is that when I walk down the street, folks will say, 'There goes the greatest hitter who ever lived.'"

Ted Williams (1918–2002)
American professional baseball player

"I remember one time I'm batting against the Dodgers in Milwaukee. They lead, two to one. It's the bottom of the ninth, bases loaded for us, two out, and the pitcher has a full count on me. I look over to the Dodger dugout, and they're all in street clothes."

Bob Uecker (b. 1935)
American baseball player and sportscaster

"The best part of playing for the Indians is that you don't have road trips to Cleveland."

Ken "Hawk" Harrelson (b. 1941)
American baseball player and sportscaster

"I could never play in New York. The first time I ever came into a game there, I got into the bullpen car and they told me to lock the doors."

Mike Flanagan (b. 1951)
American professional baseball player

"If you're knocked down, you can't lose your guts. You need to play with supreme confidence or else you'll lose again, and then losing becomes a habit."

Joe Paterno (b. 1926)
American college football coach

"Man is a wanting animal—as soon as one of his needs is satisfied, another appears in its place. This process is unending. It continues from birth to death."

Douglas McGregor (1906–1964)
American management writer

"We never had enough food. But at least I could beat on other kids and steal their lunch money and buy myself something to eat. But I couldn't steal a father. I couldn't steal a father's hug when I needed one. I couldn't steal a father's whipping when I needed one."

Vincent Edward "Bo" Jackson (b. 1962)
American professional baseball and football player

"When I was a kid, I used to imagine animals running under my bed. I told my dad and he solved the problem quickly. He cut the legs off my bed."

Lou Brock (b. 1939)
American professional baseball player

"Every morning in Africa, a gazelle awakens. It knows it must run faster than the lion or it will be killed. Every morning in Africa, a lion awakens. It knows it must run faster than the gazelle or it will starve. It does not matter whether you are a lion or a gazelle. When the sun comes up, you'd better be running."

Anonymous

"Nothing average ever stood as a monument to progress. When progress is looking for a partner it doesn't turn to those who believe they are only average. It turns instead to those who are forever searching and striving to become the best they possibly can. If we seek the average level we cannot hope to achieve a high level of success. Our only hope is to avoid being a failure."

A. Lou Vickery (b. 1941)
American business writer

"Ain't no man can avoid being born average, but there ain't no man got to be common."

Leroy Robert "Satchel" Paige (1904–1982)
American professional baseball player

"You know you're having a bad day when the fifth inning rolls around, and they drag the warning track."

Mike Flanagan (b. 1951)
American professional baseball player

"In order that people may be happy in their work, these three things are needed: They must be for it. They must not do too much of it. And they must have a sense of success in it."

John Ruskin (1819–1900)
English art critic and historian

"I'd like to see the fairways more narrow. Then everybody would have to play from the rough, not just me."

Seve Ballesteros (b. 1957)
Spanish professional golfer

"There are no traffic jams when you go the extra mile."

Anonymous

"Don't cross this field unless you can do it in 9.9 seconds.
The bull can do it in 10."

Sign in Midwest U.S. pasture

"Did is a word of achievement, Won't is a word of retreat,
Might is a word of bereavement, Can't is a word of defeat,
Ought is a word of duty, Try is a word each hour,
Will is a word of beauty, Can is a word of power."

Anonymous

"Courage is doing what you're afraid to do. There can be no courage unless you're scared."

Eddie Rickenbacker (1890–1973)
American aviator

"Courage is doing something you need to do that might get you hurt."

Bobby Bowden (b. 1930)
head football coach, Florida State University

"The best parachute folders are those who jump themselves."

Anonymous

"We know nothing about motivation. All we can do is write books about it."

Peter Drucker (b. 1909)
American business philosopher and author

"The only prize much cared for by the powerful is power. The prize of the general is not a bigger tent, but command."

Oliver Wendell Holmes, Jr. (1841–1935)
American jurist

"Success is getting what you want; happiness is wanting what you get."

Anonymous

"Happiness is not money and it's not fame and it's not power. Those are nice, but they only last a finger snap. Happiness is a good wife, a good family, and good health."

Bobby Bowden (b. 1930)
head football coach, Florida State University

"Be happy. If you're successful, but unhappy, that's emptiness."

John McEnroe (b. 1959)
American professional tennis player

"All you need for happiness is a good gun, a good horse, and a good wife."

Daniel Boone (1734–1820)
American frontiersman

"A good coach needs a patient wife, a loyal dog, and a great quarterback—not necessarily in that order."

Bud Grant (b. 1927)
American professional football coach

"You know what happiness is? Happiness in sports is winning on the road."

Al McGuire (1928–2001)
American college basketball coach and sportscaster

"Notice the difference between what happens when a man says to himself, 'I have failed three times,' and what happens when he says, 'I am a failure.'"

S. I. Hayakawa (1906–1992)
American semanticist and U.S. Senator

"I've missed more than 9000 shots in my career. I've lost almost 300 games; 26 times I've been trusted to take the game-winning shot and missed. I've failed over and over and over again in my life. And this is why I succeeded."

Michael Jordan (b. 1963)
American professional basketball player

"Encouragement after censure is as the sun after a shower."

Johann Wolfgang von Goethe (1749–1832)
German poet and dramatist

"A ballplayer's got to be kept hungry to become a big leaguer. That's why no boy from a rich family ever made the big leagues."

Joe DiMaggio (1914–1999)
American professional baseball player

"Adversity causes some men to break; others to break records.

William A. Ward
American author

"Once a guy starts wearing silk pajamas, it's hard to get up early."

Eddie Arcaro (1916–1997)
American jockey

"I like players to be married and in debt. That's the way you motivate them."

Ernie Banks (b. 1931)
American baseball player and coach

"A good horse should be seldom spurred."

Thomas Fuller (1608–1661)
English clergyman and author

"Don't fear failure so much that you refuse to try new things. The saddest summary of a life contains three descriptions: could have, might have, and should have."

Louis E. Boone (b. 1941)
American educator and business writer

Chapter 12

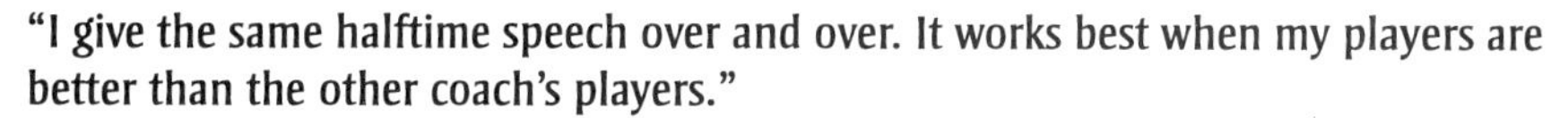

Communication

"I give the same halftime speech over and over. It works best when my players are better than the other coach's players."

Chuck Mills (b. 1928)
American college football coach

"Put it to them briefly so they will read it; clearly, so they will appreciate it; picturesquely, so they will remember it; and, above all, accurately, so they will be guided by its light."

Joseph Pulitzer (1847–1911)
American journalist and publisher

"Good shot, bad luck, and hell are the five basic words to be used in a game of tennis."

Virginia Graham (1912–1998)
American author and lecturer

"People who read tabloids deserve to be lied to."

Jerry Seinfeld (b. 1954)
American comedian

"To me, giving speeches is like hosting parties: Your role is to make everybody comfortable."

Jim McCann
president, 1-800-Flowers

"The fellow that agrees with everything you say is either a fool or he is getting ready to skin you."

Frank McKinney "Kin" Hubbard (1868–1930)
American humorist

"To improve communications, work not on the utterer, but the recipient."

Peter Drucker (b. 1909)
American business philosopher and author

"I do not object to people looking at their watches when I am speaking. But I strongly object when they start shaking them to make certain they are still going."

Lord Birkett (1883–1962)
British jurist

"Now on the pot, Johnny Tee."

Television announcer introducing golfer Johnny Pot
on the first tee of the Los Angeles Open

"Allen S. Sothoron pitched his initials off yesterday."

Arthur "Bugs" Baer (1876–1969)
American sportswriter and cartoonist
(after journeyman Sothoron pitched a shutout)

"Well, I see in the game in Minnesota that Terry Felton relieved himself on the mound in the second inning."

Fred White
veteran Kansas City Royals sportscaster
(noting an erroneous box score that listed the Minnesota Twins pitcher as both the starting and the relief pitcher in the same game)

"I didn't say that I didn't say it. I said that I didn't say that I said it. I want to make that very clear."

George Romney (1907–1995)
American industrialist and Governor of Michigan

"It's still embarrassing. I asked my caddie for a sand wedge, and ten minutes later he came back with a ham on rye."

Chi Chi Rodriguez (b. 1935)
Puerto Rico-born professional golfer
(on his accent)

"I can't stand whispering. Every time a doctor whispers in the hospital, next day there's a funeral."

George Bernard Shaw (1856–1950)
English playwright and social reformer

"The bases were drunk, and I painted the black with my best yakker. But blue squeezed me, and I went full. I came back with my heater, but the stick flares one the other way and chalk flies for two bases. Three earnies! Next thing I know, skipper hooks me and I'm sipping suds with the clubby."

Ed Lynch (b. 1956)
American professional baseball player
(on an unsuccessful pitching performance)

"How come we drive on parkways and park on driveways?"

Larry Anderson (b. 1952)
American professional baseball player

"How do you say 'Adios' in Spanish?"

Clay Carroll (b. 1941)
American professional baseball player

"I'm the oratorical equivalent of a blocked punt."

Hayden Fry (b. 1929)
American college football coach
(on his public speaking abilities)

"I like the way you always manage to state the obvious with a sense of real discovery."

Gore Vidal (b. 1925)
American author and dramatist

"Never answer a question, other than an offer of marriage, by saying yes or no."

Susan Chitty (b. 1929)
English writer

"A closed mouth gathers no feet."

Anonymous

"One who never asks either knows everything or nothing."

Malcolm Forbes (1919–1990)
American publisher

"Bragging may not bring happiness, but no man having caught a large fish goes home through an alley."

Anonymous

"It ain't braggin' if you can do it."

Jay Hanna "Dizzy" Dean (1910–1974)
American professional baseball player

"The Babe is here. Who's coming in second?"

Babe Didrikson Zaharias (1914–1956)
American professional golfer

"Boredom is having to listen to someone talk about himself when I want to talk about me."

Tom Paciorek (b. 1946)
American professional baseball player

"The trouble with telling a good story is that it invariably reminds the other fellow of a bad one."

Sid Caesar (b. 1922)
American actor

DECIPHERING JOCKSPEAK

Business executives communicating with potential customers who are sports enthusiasts know the importance of understanding the lingo. Among the sports catch phrases included in a recent edition of *Merriam Webster's Collegiate Dictionary* are:

chin music	four-peat	post-up
pump fake	red zone	run-and-gun
shot clock	small forward	triple-double

Chapter 13

Decision Making

"You don't save a pitcher for tomorrow. Tomorrow it may rain."

Leo Durocher (1905–1991)
American baseball player and manager

"It is only in our decisions that we are important."

Jean-Paul Sartre (1905–1980)
French philosopher, dramatist, and novelist

"All of us must become better informed. It is necessary for us to learn from others' mistakes. You will not live long enough to make them all yourself."

Hyman G. Rickover (1900–1986)
Admiral, U.S. Navy; father of the nuclear navy

"I sought advice and cooperation from all those around, but not permission."

Muhammad Ali (b. 1942)
World heavyweight boxing champion, 1964–1967, 1974–1978

"Whenever I make a bum decision, I just go out and make another."

Harry S Truman (1884–1972)
33rd president of the United States (1945–1953)

"Any time I got one of those bang-bang plays at first base, I called them out. It made the game shorter."

Tom Gorman (1919–1986)
American baseball umpire

"One of these days in your travels a guy is going to come up to you and show you a nice brand-new deck of cards on which the seal is not yet broken, and this guy is going to offer to bet you that he can make the jack of spades jump out of the deck and squirt cider in your ear. But, son, do not bet this man, for as sure as you stand there, you are going to wind up with an earful of cider."

Damon Runyon (1884–1946)
American author

"All the mistakes I ever made were when I wanted to say 'No' and said 'Yes.'"

Moss Hart (1904–1961)
American dramatist

"Assumption is the mother of screw-up."

Angelo Donghia (1934–1985)
American designer

"Take time to deliberate; but when the time for action arrives, stop thinking and go in."

Andrew Jackson (1767–1845)
7th president of the United States (1829–1837)

"There is a syndrome in sports called 'paralysis by analysis.'"

Arthur Ashe (1943–1993)
American professional tennis player

"You'll never have all the information you need to make a decision. If you did, it would be a foregone conclusion, not a decision."

David J. Mahoney, Jr. (b. 1923)
American corporate executive

"If a man mulls over a decision, they say, 'He's weighing the options.' If a woman does it, they say, 'She can't make up her mind.'"

Barbara Proctor (b. 1933)
American advertising executive

"There is always an easy solution to every human problem—neat, plausible and wrong."

H. L. Mencken (1880–1956)
American editor

"Not to decide is to decide."

Harvey Cox (b. 1929)
American author

"Never go out to meet trouble. If you will just sit still, nine cases out of ten someone will intercept it before it reaches you."

Calvin Coolidge (1872–1933)
30th president of the United States (1923–1929)

"If you bet on a horse, that's gambling. If you bet you can make three spades, that's entertainment. If you bet cotton will go up three points, that's business. See the difference?"

William F. "Blackie" Sherrod (b. 1920)
American sportswriter

"No amount of sophistication is going to allay the fact that all your knowledge is about the past and all your decisions are about the future."

Ian E. Wilson (b. 1943)
former chairman, General Electric

"When a three-engine Boeing 727 flying at 40,000 feet loses all three engines at once (under normal circumstances, the plane could glide for over 130 miles), the captain has ample time for quickly consulting with his copilot and flight engineer to get their ideas about the cause and remedy, and to discuss emergency procedures with the stewardesses. However, if a similar power loss occurred at 500 feet during a takeoff climb, the captain would be ill advised to practice such participative techniques."

J. Clayton Lafferty (1924–2001)
founder and former president,
Human Synergistics, Inc.

"In skating over thin ice, our safety is in our speed."

Ralph Waldo Emerson (1803–1882)
American essayist and poet

"You don't know what pressure is until you play for five bucks with only two in your pocket."

Lee Trevino (b. 1939)
American professional golfer

"There's no pressure here. This is a lot of fun. Pressure is when you have to go to the unemployment office to pick up a check to support four people."

George Brett (b. 1953)
American professional baseball player

"You don't concentrate on risks. You concentrate on results. No risk is too great to prevent the necessary job from getting done."

Charles E. "Chuck" Yeager (b. 1923)
American test pilot

"Know the odds of success and the consequences of failure when taking a risk."

Joe Moglia (b. 1949)
CEO, Ameritrade

"You can use all the quantitative data you can get, but you still have to distrust it and use your own intelligence and judgment."

Alvin Toffler (b. 1928)
American author

"We know what happens to people who stay in the middle of the road. They get run over."

Aneurin Bevan (1897–1960)
British politician

"There's nothing in the middle of the road but yellow stripes and dead armadillos."

James Allen "Jim" Hightower (b. 1943)
former Texas Agricultural Commissioner

"Great crises produce great men and great deeds of courage."

John F. Kennedy (1917–1963)
35th president of the United States (1961–1963)

"When you cannot make up your mind which of two evenly balanced courses of action you should take—choose the bolder."

W. J. Slim (1891–1970)
General, British Army

"The fox that waited for the chickens to fall off their perch died of hunger."

Greek proverb

"When you come to a fork in the road, take it."

Yogi Berra (b. 1925)
American baseball player and manager

Part 4

Building a Competitive Team

Chapter 14

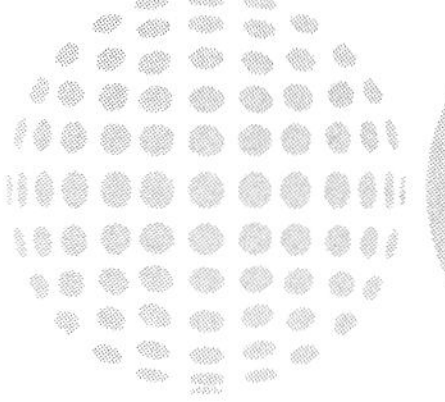

THE ORGANIZATION

"Baseball isn't a business; it's more like a disease."

Walter O'Malley (1903–1979)
American professional baseball club owner

"When I was a little boy, I wanted to be a baseball player and join the circus. With the Yankees I've accomplished both."

Graig Nettles (b.1944)
American professional baseball player

"The important thing to recognize is that it takes a team, and the team ought to get credit for the wins and losses. Successes have many fathers; failures have none."

Philip Caldwell (b. 1920)
Chairman, Ford Motor Co. (1980–1985)

"The main ingredient of stardom is the rest of the team."

John Wooden (b. 1910)
American college basketball coach

"Talent wins games, but teamwork and intelligence win championships."

Michael Jordan (b. 1963)
American professional basketball player

"A player who conjugates a verb in the first person singular cannot be part of a squad; he has to conjugate the verb in the first person plural. We. We want to conquer. We are going to conquer. Using the word 'I' when you're in a group makes things complicated."

Wanderley Luxemburgo (b. 1952)
Brazilian national soccer coach

"Our team is well balanced. We have problems everywhere."

Tommy Prothro (b. 1920)
American college football coach

"Good teams become great ones when the members trust each other enough to surrender the 'me' for the 'we.'"

Phil Jackson (b. 1945)
American basketball coach

"All organizations are at least 50 percent waste—waste people, waste effort, waste space, and waste time."

Robert Townsend (1920–1998)
American business writer and former president,
Avis-Rent-A-Car, Inc.

"You don't get the breaks unless you play with the team instead of against it."

Lou Gehrig (1903–1941)
American professional baseball player

"Show me a friend in need and I'll show you a pest."

Joe E. Lewis (1902–1971)
American comedian

"A team is where a boy can prove courage on his own. A gang is where a coward goes to hide."

Mickey Mantle (1931–1995)
American professional baseball player

"A company is known by the people it keeps."

Anonymous

"Any job that has defeated two or three men in succession, even though each performed well in his previous assignments, should be deemed unfit for human beings and must be redesigned."

Peter Drucker (b. 1909)
American business philosopher and author

"I have built my organization upon fear."

Al Capone (1899–1947)
American gangster

"Every successful enterprise requires three men—a dreamer, a businessman, and an SOB."

Peter McArthur (1866–1924)
Canadian author

"Titles distinguish the mediocre, embarrass the superior, and are disgraced by the inferior."

George Bernard Shaw (1856–1950)
British playwright and social reformer

"The longer the title, the less important the job."

George McGovern (b. 1922)
American politician

"The most difficult part of getting to the top of the ladder is getting through the crowd at the bottom."

Arch Ward (1896–1955)
American sports editor

"After the verb 'to love,' 'to help' is the most beautiful verb in the world."

Bertha von Suttner (1843–1914)
Austrian novelist

"Never explain. Your friends do not need it and your enemies will not believe you anyway."

Elbert Hubbard (1856–1915)
American writer

"Every organization has a Siberia."

Warren G. Bennis (b. 1925)
American educator and business writer

"If you assign people duties without granting them any rights, you must pay them well."

Johann Wolfgang von Goethe (1749–1832)
German poet and dramatist

"The person who knows *how* will always have a job. The person who knows *why* will always be his boss."

Diane Ravitch (b. 1938)
American educator

Chapter 15

Training and Conditioning

"The grass is not, in fact, always greener on the other side of the fence. No, not at all. Fences have nothing to do with it. The grass is greenest where it is watered. When crossing over fences, carry water with you and tend the grass wherever you may be."

Robert Fulghum (b. 1937)
American author

"The will to win is important, but the will to prepare is vital."

Joe Paterno (b. 1926)
American college football coach

"I'm like a duck: calm above the water, and paddling like hell underneath."

Fred Shero (b. 1925)
Canadian-born NHL hockey player and coach

"If you train hard, you'll not only be hard, you'll be hard to beat."

Herschel Walker (b. 1962)
American professional football player

"Just remember this: No one ever won the olive wreath with an impressive training diary."

Marty Liquori (b. 1949)
American Olympic distance runner

"I just a little bit deplore that you've got to work for two years every working day to prepare for a sailboat race."

Bob Bavier (1918–2001)
America's Cup skipper

"One important key to success to self-confidence. An important key to self-confidence is preparation."

Arthur Ashe (1943–1993)
American professional tennis player

"Work only half a day. It makes no difference which half—the first 12 hours or the last 12 hours."

Kemmons Wilson (1913–2003)
American executive; founder of Holiday Inn

"One day of practice is like one day of clean living. It doesn't do you any good."

Abe Lemons (1922–2002)
American college basketball coach

"A really busy person never knows how much he weighs."

Ed Howe (1853–1937)
American journalist

"When I was little, I was big."

William "The Refrigerator" Perry (b. 1962)
American professional football player

"I won't say I'm out of condition now—but I even puff going down stairs."

Dick Gregory (b. 1932)
American comedian

"I have never yet met a healthy person who worried very much about his health, or a really good person who worried much about his own soul."

J.B.S. Haldane (1892–1964)
British scientist

"People who cannot find time for recreation are obliged sooner or later to find time for illness."

John Wanamaker (1838–1922)
American merchant

"My doctor gave me six months to live, but when I couldn't pay the bill he gave me six months more."

Walter Matthau (1920–2000)
American actor

"When I told my doctor I couldn't afford an operation, he offered to touch up my X-rays."

Henny Youngman (1906–1998)
American comedian

"The only reason I would take up jogging is so that I could hear heavy breathing again."

Erma Bombeck (1927–1996)
American writer and humorist

"I believe every human has a finite number of heartbeats. I don't intend to waste any of mine running around doing exercise."

Neil Armstrong (b. 1930)
American astronaut

"Exercise daily. Eat wisely. Die anyway."

Anonymous

"I don't jog. If I die, I want to be sick."

Abe Lemons (1922–2002)
American college basketball coach

"A man too busy to take care of his health is like a mechanic too busy to take care of his tools."

Spanish proverb

"Casey [Stengel] said, 'This guy's going to be better than DiMaggio.' It didn't happen. God gave me a great body, and I didn't take care of it."

Mickey Mantle (1931–1995)
American professional baseball player

"Everyone who roomed with Mickey [Mantle] said he took five years off their careers."

Waite Hoyt (1899–1984)
American professional baseball player

"I don't room with him [Babe Ruth]. I room with his suitcase."

Ping Bodie (1887–1961)
American professional baseball player

"The only way to keep your health is to eat what you don't want, drink what you don't like, and do what you'd rather not."

Mark Twain (1835–1910)
American author

"Better make it six. I can't eat eight."

attributed to Yogi Berra (b. 1925)
American baseball player and manager
(when asked by a waitress whether he wanted his pizza cut into six or eight slices)

"I get my exercise acting as a pallbearer to my friends who exercise."

Chauncy Depew (1834–1928)
American attorney and speaker

"Early to rise and early to bed makes a man healthy and wealthy and dead."

James Thurber (1894–1961)
American writer

"If you resolve to give up smoking, drinking, and loving, you don't actually live longer; it just seems longer."

Clement Freud (b. 1924)
English author

"If a horse can't eat it, I don't want to play on it."

Dick Allen (b. 1942)
American professional baseball player
(complaining about artificial turf)

"Drink the first. Sip the second slowly. Skip the third."

Knute Rockne (1888–1931)
Norwegian-born college football coach

"Part of the secret of success in life is to eat what you like and let the food fight it out inside."

Mark Twain (1835–1910)
American author

"He was eating things we wouldn't even go swimming with in Alabama."

Charley Hannah (b. 1955)
American professional football player
(on dining with Tampa Bay Buccaneers
teammate Abe Gibron)

"They didn't hesitate: Wendy's, McDonald's, Pizza Hut, and Burger King."

Jackie Berning
University of Colorado sports nutritionist
(asking Denver Bronco NFL team players to identify
the four basic food groups)

"If bumblebee leavings and stump paste are so good for you, why can't any of those guys [in health-food stores] grow full beards?"

Calvin Trillin (b.1935)
American author and food critic

"Health nuts are going to feel stupid someday, lying in hospitals dying of nothing."

Redd Fox (1922–2001)
American comedian

"When we lose, I eat. When we win, I eat. I also eat when we're rained out."

Tommy Lasorda (b. 1927)
American baseball manager

"A waist is a terrible thing to mind."

Terry Forster (b. 1952)
American professional baseball player

"Eat, drink, and be merry, for tomorrow ye diet."

Lewis C. Henry (1885–1941)
U.S. Congressman

"I've been on a diet for two weeks and all I've lost is two weeks."

Totie Fields (1930–1978)
American comedienne

"Too much food in America, man. We got so much food in America, we're allergic to food, allergic to food! Hungry people aren't allergic to [anything.] Do you think anybody in Rwanda got a lactose intolerance?"

Chris Rock (b. 1965)
American actor and comedian

"You mix two jiggers of Scotch to one jigger of Metrecal. So far I've lost five pounds and my driver's license."

Rocky Bridges (b. 1927)
American baseball player and manager

"First you take a drink, then the drink takes a drink, then the drink takes you."

F. Scott Fitzgerald (1896–1940)
American writer

"If you drink, don't drive. Don't even putt."

Dean Martin (1917–1995)
American actor and comedian

"Never eat in a restaurant that's over a hundred feet off the ground and won't stand still."

Calvin Trillin (b. 1935)
American author and food critic

"When it's third and ten, you can take the milk drinkers and I'll take the whiskey drinkers every time."

Max McGee (b. 1932)
American professional football player

"Training camp is tough, and there's some pain. But it's a good life. It's better than working."

Doug Atkins (b. 1930)
American professional football player

"I would rather sandpaper a bobcat's butt in a phone booth than be tackled by Fredd."

Bryan Millard (b. 1960)
American professional football player
(on the toughness of Seattle Seahawk linebacker Fredd Young)

"I just hope I never get kicked in the groin."

John Elway (b. 1960)
former Denver Broncos quarterback
(on repeated diagrams in Denver newspapers of his ruptured biceps tendon)

"If I had known I was going to live so long, I would have taken better care of myself."

Anonymous

"If you break your leg, stop thinking about dancing and start decorating the cast."

Warren Zevon (1947–2003)
American singer-songwriter

"I don't like wallowing with pessimists."

General Colin Powell (b. 1937)
U.S. military leader and secretary of state

Chapter 16

Winning and Losing

"When you win, nothing hurts."

Joe Namath (b. 1943)
American football star

"Drive for show and putt for dough."

Al Balding (b. 1924)
Canadian professional golfer

"His driving is unbelievable. I don't go that far on my holidays."

Ian Baker-Finch (b. 1960)
Australian professional golfer
(on the long drives hit by John Daly)

"The woods are full of long drivers."

Harvey Penick (1905–1995)
American golf teacher

"Winning isn't everything; it's the only thing."

Henry "Red" Sanders (1905–1958)
American college football coach

"When I joined the Tour I studied the best players to see what they did that I didn't do. I came to the conclusion that the successful player has the Three C's: Confidence, Composure, Concentration."

Bob Toski (b. 1927)
American professional golfer

"I have a lot of money to spend and not a lot of time (to live) and I want a World Series ring."

Gene Autry (1907–1998)
American actor and former owner, California Angels baseball club

"It is a silly game where nobody wins."

Thomas Fuller (1608–1661)
English chaplain to Charles II

"Nobody remembers who came in second."

Charles Schulz (1922–2000)
American cartoonist

"There are only two places in this league: first place and no place."

Tom Seaver (b. 1944)
American professional baseball player

"If you think it's hard to meet new people, try picking up the wrong golf ball."

Jack Lemmon (1925–2001)
American actor

"I'm fairly confident that if I died tomorrow, Don would find a way to preserve me until the season was over and he had time for a nice funeral."

Dorothy Shula (1934–1991)
(wife of American professional football coach Don Shula)

"Every time you win, you're reborn; when you lose, you die a little."

George Allen (1918–1990)
American college and professional football coach

"Behold the turtle. He makes progress only when he sticks his neck out."

James Bryant Conant (1893–1978)
American chemist and educator

"There is one word in America that says it all, and that one word is, 'You never know.'"

Joaquin Andujar (b. 1952)
Dominican-born professional baseball player

"All I had to do was keep turning left."

George Robson (1907–1946)
British auto racing champion
(on winning the 1946 Indianapolis 500)

"I don't get my kicks from flirting with death. I flirt with life. It's not that I enjoy the risks, the dangers, and the challenge of the race. I enjoy the life it gives me. When I finish a race, the sky looks bluer, the grass looks greener, and the air feels fresher. It's so much better to be alive."

Jackie Stewart (b. 1939)
Scottish-born auto racer

"The crashes people remember, but drivers remember the near misses."

Mario Andretti (b. 1940)
Italian-born auto racer

"On the day of the race, a lot of people want you to sign something just before you get in the car so that they can say they got your last autograph."

A. J. Foyt (b. 1935)
American auto racer

"The toughest thing about success is that you've got to keep on being a success."

Irving Berlin (1888–1989)
American composer

"Never win 20 games, because then they'll expect you to do it every year."

Billy Loes (b. 1929)
American professional baseball player

"Failure is never final and success is never-ending. Success is a journey, not a destination."

Dr. Robert Schuller (b. 1926)
American evangelist

"Losing is an integral a part of the dance (of life) as winning. . . . Only by acknowledging the possibility of defeat can you fully experience the joy of competition."

Phil Jackson (b. 1945)
head coach, NBA champions Chicago Bulls and Los Angeles Lakers

"I've heard of guys going 0 for 15 or 0 for 25, but I was 0 for July."

Bob Aspromonte (b. 1938)
American professional baseball player

"I feel the most important requirement in success is learning to overcome failure. You must learn to tolerate it, but never accept it."

Reggie Jackson (b. 1946)
American professional baseball player

"I was hot. I was smoking 'em. I was having a good time. Even a blind pig finds an acorn sometimes."

Bill Clinton (b. 1946)
42nd president of the United States (1993–2001)
(after hitting 79 and fulfilling a lifelong golfing ambition to break 80)

"I swam my brains out."

Mark Spitz (b. 1950)
U.S. Olympic gold medalist

"Pro football is like nuclear warfare. There are no winners, only survivors."

Frank Gifford (b. 1930)
American professional football player and sportscaster

"Pro football gave me a good sense of perspective to enter politics. I'd already been booed, cheered, cut, sold, traded, and hung in effigy."

Jack Kemp (b. 1935)
American politician and former National Football League quarterback

"Baseball is almost the only orderly thing in a very unorderly world. If you get three strikes, even the best lawyer in the world can't get you off."

Bill Veeck (1914–1986)
American baseball team owner

"Hey, Ma, your bad boy done it. I told you somebody up there likes me."

Rocky Graziano (1921–1990)
World Middleweight boxing champion, 1947–1948
(after defeating Tony Zale for the title)

"Little man whip[s] a big man every time if the little man's in the right and keeps on coming."

Texas Rangers Baseball Club motto

"To win you have to risk loss."

Jean-Claude Killy (b. 1943)
French-born professional skier

"Some days you tame the tiger. And some days the tiger has you for lunch."

Frank Edwin "Tug" McGraw (1944–2004)
American professional baseball player

"If the lion didn't bite the tamer every once in a while, it wouldn't be exciting."

Darrell Waltrip (b. 1947)
American auto racer

"The Yankees cannot lose. But I fear the Indians of Cleveland."

Ernest Hemingway (1899–1961)
American writer and journalist
(in The Old Man and the Sea*)*

"I must point out that I do not have much experience in the art of losing, and it is not something I wish to master."

Garry Kasparov (b. 1963)
International Grand Master of Chess

"Some days you're the pigeon and some days you're the statue."

Bernie Bickerstaff (b. 1945)
American professional basketball coach

"The opera ain't over till the fat lady sings."

Dan Cook (b. 1942)
American sports broadcaster and writer

"It isn't over till it's over."

Yogi Berra (b. 1925)
American baseball player and manager

"If you see a defensive team with dirt and mud on their backs, they've had a bad day."

John Madden (b. 1936)
American football coach and sports analyst

"Even Napoleon had his Watergate."

Danny Ozark (b. 1923)
American baseball player and manager
(following a ten-game losing streak)

"People don't seem to understand that it's a damn war out there."

Jimmy Connors (b. 1952)
American professional tennis player

"We have no time for the philosophy of waiting. We play to win these games, and to win you must attack, attack, attack."

Daniel Amokachi (b. 1972)
member, 1998 Nigerian World Cup team

"I say to our enemies, 'We are coming. God may show you mercy. We will not.'"

John McCain (b. 1936)
American war hero and U.S. Senator

"Sectional football games have the glory and the despair of war, and when a Texas team takes the field against a foreign state, it is an army with banners."

John Steinbeck (1902–1968)
American author

"In the East, college football is a cultural exercise. On the West Coast, it is a tourist attraction. In the Midwest, it is cannibalism. But in the Deep South it is religion, and Saturday is the Holy Day."

Marino Casem (b. 1934)
former athletic director and head football coach,
Alcorn State University

"I'd rather be lucky than good."

Vernon "Lefty" Gomez (1908–1989)
American professional baseball player

"Bob Gibson is the luckiest pitcher I ever saw. He always pitches when the other team doesn't score any runs."

Tim McCarver (b. 1941)
American baseball player and sportscaster

"I think it's a good idea."

John McKay (b. 1923)
American college and professional football coach
(when, following a loss, a sportswriter asked him
"How do you feel about your team's execution?")

"My biggest thrill was the night Elgin Baylor and I combined for 73 points in Madison Square Garden. Elgin had 71 of them."

"Hot Rod" Hundley (b. 1934)
American basketball player

"Show me a good loser and I'll show you a loser."

Anonymous

"Show me a good and gracious loser, and I'll show you a failure."

Knute Rockne (1888–1931)
Norwegian-born college football coach

"Musamba Bwayla is a stupid man and a hopeless player. He has a huge nose and is crosseyed. Girls hate him. He beat me because my jockstrap was too tight and because when he serves he farts, and that made me lose my concentration, for which I am famous throughout Zambia."

Lighton Ndefwayl
Zambian tennis player
(after losing a 1992 tennis match to fellow
Zambian Musumba Bwayla)

"He [Jimmy Connors] has one weakness. He can never say his opponent played well. That's why it feels good to beat him and that's why other players would rather beat him than any other player."

Bjorn Borg (b. 1956)
Swedish professional tennis player

"If there's a good loser in boxing, I'd like to fight him every week."

Gene Fulmer (b. 1931)
World middleweight boxing champion, 1957, 1959–1962

"I hate losing more than I love winning."

Jimmy Connors (b. 1952)
American professional tennis player

"For all the sad words of tongue and pen, the saddest are these: 'It might have been.'"

John Greenleaf Whittier (1807–1892)
American poet

"A tie game is like kissing your sister."

Eddie Erdelatz (1913–1966)
American college football coach

"The minute you start talking about what you're going to do if you lose, you have lost."

George P. Schultz (b. 1920)
American industrialist and U.S. secretary of state

"Failure is success if we learn from it."

Malcolm Forbes (1919–1990)
American publisher

"Some days you're a bug. Some days you're a windshield."

Price Cobb (b. 1954)
American race-car driver (after winning a 1988 race)

"I zigged when I should have zagged."

Jack Roper
American boxer
(explaining being knocked out by Joe Louis in a 1939 fight)

"And never quit. Never, never, never."

H. Ross Perot (b. 1930)
American computer industry executive and philanthropist

"If at first you don't succeed, try, try again. Then quit. There's no use being a damn fool about it."

W. C. Fields (1880–1946)
American actor and comedian

"You may have a fresh start any moment you choose, for this thing we call 'failure' is not the falling down, but the staying down."

Henry Ford (1863–1947)
American auto maker

"Pitching is the art of instilling fear."

Sandy Koufax (b. 1935)
American professional baseball player

"My goal was to get out of there alive. Yeah, it's hard to hit when you're laughing. It's harder to hit when you're dead."

John Kruk (b. 1961)
Philadelphia Phillies first baseman
(on his memorable 1993 All Star Game plate appearance against fireballing southpaw Randy Johnson. Johnson's first pitch, a blazing fastball, sailed above Kruk's head and Kruk struck out by fleeing the batter's box on each of the next two pitches.)

"I couldn't have driven Miss Daisy home today."

Andy Van Slyke (b. 1960)
American professional baseball player
on a disappointing hitting performance)

"Any team can have a bad century."

Tom Treblehorn
Chicago Cubs manager (on the Cubs' inability to win a pennant since 1945 or a World Series since 1908)

"Some football teams almost always have losing seasons. That's not an option in business."

Joe Moglia (b. 1949)
CEO, Ameritrade

"In my opinion, if we are going to have a good season, we have to put together more back-to-back wins."

Jim Fassel (b. 1949)
former head coach, New York Giants professional football club
(on the following year's team prospects)

"You never fail until you quit trying."

Florence Griffith-Joyner (1960–1998)
U.S. Olympic triple gold medalist in field events

"We wuz robbed."

Joe Jacobs
American boxing manager
(after his fighter, Max Schmeling, lost the heavyweight title in 1932 to Jack Sharkey on a foul)

"I never get tired of losing. Losing is not the worst thing that can happen."

Red Klotz (b. 1921)
American basketball coach
(whose Washington Generals haven't beaten the Harlem Globetrotters since 1971, more than 13,000 games ago)

"Rule Number 1 is don't sweat the small stuff.
Rule Number 2 is it's all small stuff.
And if you can't fight and you can't flee, flow."

Robert S. Eliot (b. 1929)
American cardiologist

"Defeat is worse than death, because you have to live with defeat."

Vince Lombardi (1913–1970)
American professional football coach

"When you're playing for the national championship, it's not a matter of life or death. It's more important than that."

Duffy Daugherty (1915–1987)
American college football coach

"Things were so bad in Chicago last summer that by the fifth inning we were selling hot dogs to go."

Ken Brett (1948–2003)
American professional baseball player

"One thing you learn as a Cubs fan: When you bought your ticket, you could bank on seeing the bottom of the ninth."

Joe Garagiola (b. 1926)
American baseball player and sportscaster

"A man is not finished when he is defeated. He is finished when he quits."

Richard M. Nixon (1913–1994)
37th president of the United States (1969–1974)

"We've been in the cellar so long we've got watermarks."

Claude Robbins "Chena" Gilstrap
American college football coach

"I never lost a game. I just ran out of time."

Bobby Layne (1926–1986)
American professional football player

"There are days when it takes all you've got just to keep up with the losers."

Robert Orben (b. 1927)
American humorist

"Well, that kind of puts the damper on even a Yankee win."

Phil Rizzuto (b. 1918)
American baseball player and broadcaster
(on hearing the 1978 news bulletin that
Pope Paul VI had died)

"No matter how good you are, you're going to lose one third of your games. No matter how bad you are, you're going to win one third of your games. It's the other third that makes the difference."

Tommy Lasorda (b. 1927)
American baseball manager

"There are still over 600 million Chinese who don't care if we win or lose."

John McKay (b. 1923)
American college and professional football coach

"The important thing is to learn a lesson every time you lose."

John McEnroe (b. 1959)
American professional tennis player

"Security is mostly a superstition. It does not exist in nature. Life is either a daring adventure or nothing."

Helen Keller (1880–1968)
American essayist and lecturer

"Sometimes the light at the end of the tunnel is an oncoming train."

Lou Holtz (b. 1937)
American college football coach

"Our greatest glory is not in never failing but in rising up every time we fail."

Ralph Waldo Emerson (1803–1882)
American essayist and poet

"Hitting is timing. Pitching is upsetting timing."

Warren Spahn (1921–2003)
American professional baseball player

"The pitcher has got only a ball. I've got a bat. So the percentage in weapons is in my favor and I let the fellow with the ball do the fretting."

Hank Aaron (b. 1934)
American professional baseball player

"The way to catch a knuckleball is to wait until the ball stops rolling and then pick it up."

Bob Uecker (b. 1935)
American baseball player and sportscaster

"There are two theories on hitting the knuckleball. Unfortunately, neither of them works."

Charley Lau (1933–1984)
American baseball hitting instructor

"It's like watching Mario Andretti park a car."

Ralph Kiner (b. 1922)
American baseball player
(describing Hall-of-Fame pitcher Phil Niekro's knuckleball)

"If you are caught on a golf course during a storm and are afraid of lightning, hold up a one iron. Not even God can hit a one iron."

Lee Trevino (b. 1939)
American professional golfer

"My reaction to anything that happens on the golf course is no reaction. There are no birdies or bogeys, no eagles or double bogeys. There are only numbers. If you can get that way, you can play this game."

Jim Colbert (b. 1941)
American professional golfer

"I find it to be the hole in one."

Groucho Marx (1895–1977)
American actor and comedian
(when asked about the toughest shot in golf)

"I found out that it's not good to talk about my troubles. Eighty percent of the people who hear them don't care and the other twenty percent are glad you're having trouble."

Tommy Lasorda (b. 1927)
American baseball manager

"Success is simply a matter of luck. Ask any failure."

Earl Wilson (1907–1987)
American newspaper columnist

Part 5

Managing the Twenty-First Century Athlete

Chapter 17

Education

"The road to the boardroom leads through the locker room."

David Riesman (1909–2002)
American sociologist

"Son, looks to me like you're spending too much time on one subject."

Shelby Metcalf (b. 1930)
American college basketball coach
(to a Texas A&M University varsity player whose grades for the previous semester consisted of four Fs and one D)

"Although I never played football, I made many contributions. I went to the University of Southern California in the late 1940s and took the English exams for all the Trojan linemen."

Art Buchwald (b. 1925)
American humorist

"A school without football is in danger of deteriorating into a medieval study hall."

Vince Lombardi (1913–1970)
American professional football coach

"We had a lot of nicknames—Scarface, Blackie, Toothless—and those were just the cheerleaders."

Frank Layden (b. 1931)
American professional basketball coach
(on his Brooklyn high school)

"The studying is a lot more words. The playbook is a lot more pictures."

Chris Darkins (b. 1974)
American football player
(on the difference between his academic work at the University of Minnesota and learning football plays at an NFL minicamp)

"The trouble with being educated is that it takes a long time; it uses up the better part of your life and, when you are finished, what you know is that you would have benefited more by going into banking."

Philip K. Dick (1928–1982)
American science fiction writer

"I couldn't care less about all those fiction stories about what happened in the year 1500 or 1600. Half of them aren't even true."

John Daly (b. 1958)
American professional golfer (on his lack of interest in world literature as a University of Arkansas student)

"I know a lot of people who think I'm dumb. Well, at least I ain't no educated fool."

Leon Spinks (b. 1953)
World heavyweight boxing champion, 1978–1979

"Baseball players are smarter than football players. How often do you see a baseball team penalized for too many men on the field?"

Jim Bouton (b. 1939)
American baseball player and author

"I took a little English, a little math, some science, a few hubcaps, and some wheel covers."

Gates Brown (b. 1939)
American professional baseball player

"I never fail to be amused by those figures of speech that the dictionary labels *oxymorons:* those combinations of contradictory terms like jumbo shrimp, sanitary landfill, and military intelligence. But my favorite is student athlete."

Louis E. Boone (b. 1941)
American educator and business writer

"It was like a heart transplant. We tried to implant college in him but his head rejected it."

Barry Switzer (b. 1937)
American college football coach
(on a football recruit who withdrew from Oklahoma University)

"Some people who don't say ain't ain't eating."

Jay Hanna "Dizzy" Dean (1910–1974)
American professional baseball player

"We're trying to build a university our football team can be proud of."

George L. Cross (b. 1905)
former president, Oklahoma University

"An athlete who does not graduate is grossly underpaid as an entertainer. One who graduates is overpaid."

Joe Paterno (b. 1926)
American college football coach

"I know I'm only road kill on the highway to reform."

Robert Bowlsby (b. 1952)
Northern Iowa University athletic director
(speaking in opposition to sweeping athletic reforms approved by university presidents during the early 1990s)

"I never graduated. I was there for only two terms—Truman's and Eisenhower's."

Alex Karras (b.1935)
American football player and actor

"Without education, you're not going anywhere in the world."

Malcolm X (1925–1965)
American black nationalist and religious leader

"I quit school in the fifth grade because of pneumonia. Not because I had it, but because I couldn't spell it."

Rocky Graziano (1921–1990)
World middleweight boxing champion, 1947–1948

"It's a good thing I stayed in Cincinnati for four years; it took me that long to learn how to spell it."

Rocky Bridges (b. 1927)
American baseball player and manager

"I think the world is run by C students."

Al McGuire (1928–2001)
American college basketball coach and sportscaster

"True terror is to wake up one morning and discover that your high school class is running the country."

Kurt Vonnegut, Jr. (b. 1922)
American author

"From your parents you learn love and laughter and how to put one foot in front of the other. But when books are opened you discover that you have wings."

Helen Hayes (1900–1993)
American actress

"A college degree is not going to help you sink those two footers."

Johnny Miller (b. 1947)
American professional golfer (explaining his decision to drop out of college to join the PGA tour)

"Life is my college. May I graduate well, and earn some honors."

Louisa May Alcott (1832–1888)
American author

"The purpose of education is to replace an empty mind with an open one."

Malcolm S. Forbes (1919–1990)
American publisher

"When you stop learning, stop listening, stop looking and asking questions, always new questions, then it is time to die."

Lillian Smith (1897–1966)
American author

"I hear and I forget. I see and I remember. I do and I understand."

Confucius (551?- 479? B.C.E.)
Chinese philosopher and teacher

"The only president who's ever been fired at Alabama was against football. Any new president cuts his teeth on it, and he better be for it. Because if he's not, they won't win, and if they don't win, he'll get fired."

Paul W. "Bear" Bryant (1913–1983)
American college football coach

"He who has once burnt his mouth always blows his soup."

German proverb

"Our minds are lazier than our bodies."

Francois, Duc de la Rochefoucauld (1613–1680)
French writer and moralist

"The Good Lord was good to me. He gave me a strong body, a good right arm, and a weak mind."

Jay Hanna "Dizzy" Dean (1910–1974)
American professional baseball player

"It's what you learn after you know it all that counts."

John Wooden (b. 1910)
American college basketball coach

"*Intern* is French for slave."

Bill Cosby (b. 1937)
American actor and comedian

"I never let my schooling interfere with my education."

Mark Twain (1835–1910)
American writer

"You can observe a lot by just watching."

Yogi Berra (b. 1925)
.American baseball player and manager

"The man who is too old to learn was probably always too old to learn."

Henry S. Hasskins
American economist

"Every man is a damn fool for at least five minutes every day; wisdom consists in not exceeding the limit."

Elbert Hubbard (1856–1915)
American writer

"Nothing in life is to be feared. It is only to be understood."

Marie Curie (1867–1934)
French chemist

"Experience is a great advantage. The problem is that when you get the experience, you're too damned old to do anything about it."

Jimmy Connors (b. 1946)
American professional tennis player

"Lord, deliver me from the man who never makes a mistake, and also from the man who makes the same mistake twice."

Dr. William J. Mayo (1861–1939)
founder, Mayo Clinic

"There are three ingredients in the good life: learning, earning, and yearning."

Christopher Morley (1890–1957)
American writer

"I had a friend with a lifetime contract. After two bad years, the university president called him into his office and pronounced him dead."

Bob Devaney (1905–1997)
American college football coach and athletic director

"If you're a coach, NFL stands for 'Not for Long.'"

Jerry Glanville (b. 1941)
former NFL coach and TV commentator

THE SLAM DUNK! COURSE

Forget the old jokes about Basket Weaving 101 and other infamous courses widely thought to be taught so that athletes could maintain their eligibility. The University of Georgia has moved to new heights (or depths). Former Georgia assistant coach Jim Harrick Jr. took no chances in his hoops coaching class that he taught back in the Fall of 2001. Following an NCCA probe into alleged improprieties (that led to the dismissal of both head coach Jim Harrick and his son), the university released a copy of the final exam. You probably won't be shocked to learn that everyone in the class got an A—even the three students who failed to show up for the 20-question multiple choice final.

University of Georgia

Coaching Principles and Strategies of Basketball

FINAL EXAM

1. How many goals are on a basketball court?
   A. 1
   B. 2
   C. 3
   D. 4
2. How many players are allowed to play at one time on any one team in a regulation game?
   A. 2
   B. 3
   C. 4
   D. 5
3. In what league to [sic] the Georgia Bulldogs compete?
   A. ACC
   B. Big Ten
   C. SEC
   D. Pac 10
4. What is the name of the coliseum where the Georgia Bulldogs play?
   A. Cameron Indoor Arena
   B. Stegeman Coliseum
   C. Carrier Dome
   D. Pauley Pavillion
5. How many halves are in a college basketball game?
   A. 1
   B. 2
   C. 3
   D. 4
6. How many quarters are in a high school basketball game?
   A. 1
   B. 2
   C. 3
   D. 4
7. How many points does one field goal account for in a basketball game?
   A. 1
   B. 2
   C. 3
   D. 4
8. How many points does a 3-point field goal account for in a basketball game?
   A. 1
   B. 2
   C. 3
   D. 4
9. How many officials referee a college basketball game?
   A. 2
   B. 4
   C. 6
   D. 3
10. How many teams are in the NCAA Men's Basketball National Championship Tournament?
    A. 48
    B. 64
    C. 65
    D. 32
11. What is the name of the exam which all high school seniors in the State of Georgia must pass?
    A. Eye Exam
    B. How Do The Grits Taste Exam
    C. Bug Control Exam
    D. Georgia Exit Exam
12. What basic color are the uniforms the Georgia bulldogs wear in home games?
    A. White
    B. Red
    C. Black
    D. Silver
13. What basic color are the uniforms the Georgia Bulldogs wear in away games?
    A. Pink
    B. Blue
    C. Orange
    D. Red
14. How many minutes are played in a college basketball contest?
    A. 20
    B. 40
    C. 60
    D. 90

15. How many minutes are played in a high school basketball game?
    A. 15
    B. 30
    C. 32
    D. 45
16. How many fouls is a player allowed to have in one basketball game before fouling out in that game?
    A. 3
    B. 5
    C. 7
    D. 0
17. If you go on to become a huge coaching success, to whom will you tribute [sic] the credit?
    A. Mike Krzyzewski
    B. Bobby Knight
    C. John Wooden
    D. Jim Harrick Jr.
18. In your opinion, who is the best Division I assistant coach in the country?
    A. Ron Jursa [sic]
    B. John Pelphrey
    C. Jim Harrick Jr.
    D. Steve Wojciechowski

Sources: Lon Johnson, "Ex-Georgia Assistant's Exam Laughable; Can You Pass?" USA Today, *March 3, 2004; downloaded from http://www.usatoday.com/sports/collegemensbasketball; Neal McCready and Thomas Murphy, "Harrick Jr. Defends the Final Exam of His Class,"* Mobile Register, *March 13, 2004, p. C3; "Slam Dunk!"* People, *March 22, 2004, p. 119; exam released by the University of Georgia.*

Chapter 18

The Opposite Sex (And Other Distractions)

"Going to bed with a woman never hurt a ballplayer. It's staying up all night looking for them that does you in."

Casey Stengel (1891–1975)
American baseball manager

"I know ball players who would have trouble with a rule that says no sex *during* a game."

Jim Bouton (b. 1939)
American baseball player and author

"Fifty percent of life in the NBA is sex. The other 50 percent is money."

Dennis Rodman (b. 1961)
American basketball player

"My wife doesn't care what I do when I'm away, as long as I don't have a good time."

Lee Trevino (b. 1939)
American professional golfer

"Open up a ballplayer's head and you know what you'd find? A lot of little broads and a jazz band."

Mayo Smith (1915–1977)
American baseball manager

"Never go to bed mad. Stay up and fight."

Phyllis Diller (b. 1917)
American comedienne

"I think that I would still rather score a touchdown on a particular day than make love to the prettiest girl in the United States."

Paul Hornung (b. 1935)
American football player

"My wife dresses to kill. She cooks the same way."

Henny Youngman (1906–1998)
American comedian

"He had the sort of face that makes you realize God does have a sense of humor."

Bill Bryson (b. 1951)
American writer

"Large increases in cost with questionable increases in performance can be tolerated only for race horses and fancy women."

Lord Kelvin (1824–1907)
English scientist; president of the Royal Society (1890–1895)

"A woman who strives to be like a man lacks ambition."

Mae Jemison (b. 1956)
American astronaut and physicist
(first African-American female Space Shuttle astronaut)

"I got traded for a girl. It can't get any worse than that."

Keith English (b. 1974)
American minor league baseball player
(on being traded for Ila Borders, the first woman to pitch in a regular-season professional baseball game)

"I thought he was nuts."

Melissa Raglin
12-year-old Boca Raton, Florida, Youth League catcher
(on the umpire who asked her if she were wearing a league-required protective groin cup)

"The most romantic thing any woman ever said to me in bed was 'Are you sure you're not a cop?'"

Larry Brown (b. 1941)
American professional basketball coach

"Golf and sex are about the only things you can enjoy without being good at it."

Jimmy Demaret (1910–1983)
American professional golfer

"I have finally mastered what to do with the second tennis ball. Having small hands, I was becoming terribly self-conscious about keeping it in a can in the car while I served the first one. I noted some women tucked the second ball just inside the elastic leg of their tennis panties. I tried, but found the space already occupied by a leg. Now I simply drop the second ball down my cleavage, giving me a chest that often stuns my opponent throughout an entire set."

Erma Bombeck (1927–1996)
American writer and humorist

"I'll take the two-stoke penalty, but I'll be damned if I'll play it where it lays."

Elaine Johnson (b. 1915)
Canadian amateur golfer
(after her ball landed in her bra)

"When women kiss it always reminds one of prizefighters shaking hands."

H.L. Mencken (1880–1956)
American editor

"My wife wanted a big diamond."

Mookie Wilson (b. 1956)
American professional baseball player
(on why his wedding was held at a ballpark)

"Look at him! When I married him, he was a Greek god. Now he's a big fat Greek."

Babe Didrikson Zaharias (1914–1956)
American professional golfer (on husband George)

"What's the difference between a boyfriend and a husband? About 30 pounds."

Unknown

"Never get married in the morning, because you never know who you'll meet that night."

Paul Hornung (b. 1935)
American professional football player

"A man can have two, maybe three love affairs while he's married. After that, it's cheating."

Yves Montand (1921–1992)
French actor

"My toughest fight was with my first wife."

Muhammad Ali (b. 1942)
World heavyweight boxing champion, 1964–1967, 1974–1978

"I don't think I'll get married again. I'll just find a woman I don't like and give her a house."

Lewis Grizzard (1946–1994)
American humorist

"It sure didn't make me the million dollars people said it would, but it sure made my ex-wife unhappy."

Bobby Unser (b. 1934)
American auto racing champion
(on winning the Indianapolis 500)

"Love, the quest; marriage, the conquest; divorce, the inquest."

Helen Rowland (1876–1950)
English author

"You never realize how short a month is until you pay alimony."

John Barrymore (1882–1942)
American actor

"It wasn't exactly a divorce—I was traded."

Tim Conway (b. 1933)
American actor and comedian

Chapter 19

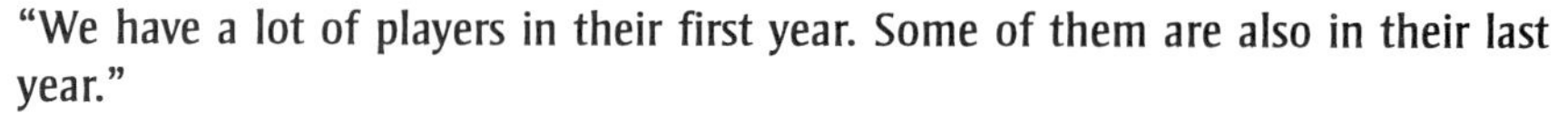

Rookies and Veterans

"We have a lot of players in their first year. Some of them are also in their last year."

Bill Walsh (b. 1931)
American professional football coach

"Don't try to go too fast. Learn your job. Don't ever talk until you know what you're talking about. If you want to get along, go along."

Sam Rayburn (1882–1961)
Speaker of the U.S. House of Representatives
(1940–1947, 1949–1953, 1955–1961)

"I am not young enough to know everything."

James Matthew Barrie (1860–1937)
Scottish novelist and dramatist

"When you're green, you're growing. When you're ripe, you rot."

Ray Kroc (1902–1984)
founder, McDonald's Corp.

"They're like tomatoes. When you get them they're green, and you want to bring them along until they're just ripe—you know, firm and ripe. They can't get mushy. Sometimes seniors go to seed."

Frank Howard (b. 1936)
American university athletic director
(on college football players)

"Wise men learn by other men's mistakes, fools by their own."

Proverb

"The trees that are slow to grow bear the best fruit."

Jean Moliere (1622–1673)
French actor and dramatist

"I'm now at an age where I've got to prove I'm just as good as I never was."

Rex Harrison (1908–1990)
English actor

"This guy is so old that the first time he had athlete's foot, he used Absorbine Sr."

Bob Costas (b. 1952)
American sportscaster
(on 45-year-old New York Yankee pitcher Tommy John)

"I forgot to put in one clause: I don't have to play when the temperature is lower than my age."

Carlton Fisk (b. 1947)
American professional baseball player
(on signing a new Chicago White Sox contract in 1990 at 42)

"It has options through the year 2020—or until the last Rocky movie is made."

Dan Quisenberry (1953–1998)
American professional baseball player
(on his contract)

"First your legs go. Then you lose your reflexes. Then you lose your friends."

Willie Pep (b. 1922)
World featherweight boxing champion, 1942–1948, 1949–1950

"I think it's wonderful you could all be here for the 43rd anniversary of my 39th birthday. We decided not to light the candles this year: We were afraid Pan Am would mistake it for a runway."

Bob Hope (1903–2003)
British-born actor and comedian
(on his 82nd birthday)

"You can't turn back the clock. But you can wind it up again."

Bonnie Prudden (b. 1914)
American physical fitness proponent

"Things do not change; we change."

Henry David Thoreau (1817–1862)
American naturalist and writer

"The four stages of man are infancy, childhood, adolescence, and obsolescence."

Art Linkletter (b. 1912)
Canadian-born radio and TV show host

"I refuse to admit that I am more than 52, even if that does make my sons illegitimate."

attributed to Lady Astor (1879–1964)
(Nancy Witcher Langhorne, Viscountess Astor)
English political leader

"The older they get, the better they were when they were younger."

Jim Bouton (b. 1939)
American baseball player and author

"Years ago we discovered the exact point, the dead center of middle age. It occurs when you are too young to take up golf and too old to rush up to the net."

Franklin P. Adams (1881–1960)
American journalist and humorist

"The difference between a job and a career is the difference between 40 and 60 hours a week."

Robert Frost (1874–1963)
American poet

"From little league sports up to the professional ranks, the athlete's role is fixated in institutionalized adolescence."

Harry Edwards (b. 1942)
American sociologist

"You can only be young once, but you can be immature forever."

Larry Anderson (b. 1953)
American professional baseball player

"The old order changeth, yielding place to new."

Alfred, Lord Tennyson (1809–1892)
English poet

"You spend a good piece of your life gripping a baseball and in the end it turns out that it was the other way around all the time."

Jim Bouton (b. 1939)
American baseball player and author

"When I grow up I want to be a little boy."

Joseph Heller (1923–1999)
American writer

Chapter

20

The Aging Athlete

"I don't want to achieve immortality by being inducted into baseball's Hall of Fame. I want to achieve immortality by not dying."

Leo Durocher (1905–1991)
American baseball player and manager

"The athlete approaches the end of his playing days the way old people approach death. But the athlete differs from the old person in that he must continue living. Behind all the years of practice and all the hours of glory waits that inexorable terror of living without the game."

Bill Bradley (b. 1943)
American professional basketball player and former U.S. Senator

"Tennis is a young man's game. Until you're 25, you can play singles. From 25 to 35, you should play doubles. I won't tell you exactly how old I am, but when I played, there were 28 men on the court just on my side of the net."

George Burns (1896–1996)
American comedian

"When I was 40, my doctor advised me that a man in his 40s shouldn't play tennis. I heeded his advice carefully and could hardly wait until I reached 50 to start again."

Hugo L. Black (1886–1971)
Associate Justice, U.S. Supreme Court

RULES FOR LONGEVITY

1. Avoid fried meats which angry up the blood.
2. If your stomach disputes you, lie down and pacify it with cool thoughts.
3. Keep the juices flowing by jangling around gently as you move.
4. Go very light on the vices, such as carrying on in society. The social ramble ain't restful.
5. Avoid running at all times.
6. Don't look back. Something might be gaining on you.

Leroy Robert "Satchel" Paige (1904–1982)
American professional baseball player

"It is well known that the older a man grows the faster he could run as a boy."

Walter Wellesley "Red" Smith (1905–1982)
American sportswriter

"I still dream about baseball almost every night. I wake up sweating; I think I'm trying to make a comeback, but I can't run to first base."

Mickey Mantle (1931–1995)
American professional baseball player (at age 59)

"I was thinking about making a comeback until I pulled a muscle vacuuming."

Johnny Bench (b. 1947)
American professional baseball player

"There has never been a great athlete who died not knowing what pain is."

Bill Bradley (b. 1943)
American professional basketball player and former U.S. Senator

"I have to get that hit this year. I might die."

Roberto Clemente (1934–1972)
Puerto Rican-born professional baseball player (following his 3,000th hit at the end of the 1972 season and less than two months before he was killed in a plane crash)

"Like a lot of fellows around here, I have a furniture problem. My chest has fallen into my drawers."

Billy Casper (b. 1931)
American professional golfer
(on joining the PGA Seniors Tour)

"Many people's tombstones should read, 'Died at 30. Buried at 60.'"

Nicholas Murray Butler (1862–1947)
American educator

"The man who views the world at 50 the same as he did at 20 has wasted 30 years of his life."

Muhammad Ali (b. 1942)
World heavyweight boxing
champion 1964–1967, 1974–1978

"How old would you be if you didn't know how old you was?"

Leroy Robert "Satchel" Paige (1904–1982)
American professional baseball player

"I'm only 32 in the Dominican Republic."

Tim Raines (b. 1959)
American professional baseball player
(on being a 42-year-old major leaguer and the proclivity of Dominican Republic players to understate their ages on their passports)

"Age is a question of mind over matter. If you don't mind, it don't matter."

Leroy Robert "Satchel" Paige (1904–1982)
American professional baseball player

"Retire to what? I'm a golfer and a fisherman. There's nothing to retire to."

Julius Boros (1920–1994)
American professional golfer

"At my age, I'm just happy to be named the greatest living anything."

Joe DiMaggio (1914–1999)
American professional baseball player

"My health is good; it's my age that's bad."

Roy Acuff (1903–1992)
American country music singer

"First thing I do when I wake up in the morning is breathe on a mirror and hope it fogs."

Early Wynn (1920–1999)
American professional baseball player

"Well, I'll never make the mistake of turning 70 again."

Casey Stengel (1891–1975)
(on his firing as New York Yankees manager in 1960, allegedly because of his age)

"Death is a distant rumor to the young."

Andy Rooney (b. 1919)
American author and news commentator

"I can't die. It would ruin my image."

Jack LaLanne (b. 1915)
American fitness advocate

"Always go to other people's funerals; otherwise they won't come to yours."

Yogi Berra (b. 1925)
American baseball player and manager

"The best way to get praise is to die."

Italian proverb

"Errol Flynn died on a 70-foot boat with a 17-year-old girl. Walter has always wanted to go that way, but he's going to settle for a 17-footer with a 70-year-old."

Mary Elizabeth "Betty" Cronkite (b. 1940)
wife of American news commentator
Walter Cronkite (b. 1916)

"Trade a player a year too early rather than a year too late."

Branch Rickey (1881–1965)
American baseball club owner

"When you cease to make a contribution you begin to die."

Eleanor Roosevelt (1884–1962)
American humanitarian and writer

"Experience is the worst teacher; it gives the test before presenting the lesson."

Vernon Law (b. 1930)
American professional baseball player

"Middle age is when you're faced with two temptations and you choose the one that will get you home by 9 o'clock."

Ronald Reagan (1911–2004)
40th president of the United States (1981–1989)

"You've heard of the three ages of man: youth, middle-age, and 'you are looking wonderful.'"

Francis Joseph Spellman (1889–1967)
American Roman Catholic cardinal

"A sure sign of old age is when you hear 'snap, crackle, and pop' and it isn't your cereal."

Robert Orben (b. 1927)
American humorist

Twenty years a child;
20 years running wild;
20 years a mature man
—and after that, praying.

Irish proverb

"I used to be a Chippendale. Now I'm a Clydesdale."

Charles Barkley (b. 1963)
American basketball player

"After 70, if you wake up without pains, you're dead."

David Brown (b. 1917)
American film producer

"After age 70, it's patch, patch, patch."

Jimmy Stewart (1908–1997)
American actor

"At this age, I don't even buy green bananas."

Donald T. Regan (b. 1918)
U.S. Treasury Secretary during the Reagan Administration
(at age 80)

"I don't deserve this, but then, I have arthritis and I don't deserve that either."

Jack Benny (1894–1974)
American comedian (on receiving an award)

"I want to thank everybody who made this day necessary."

Yogi Berra (b. 1925)
American baseball player and manager
(addressing Yogi Berra Day crowd at Yankee Stadium)

"When you're too old to chase other things, you can always chase golf balls."

Anonymous

"To retire is the beginning of death."

Pablo Casals (1876–1973)
Spanish conductor and composer

"I knew when my career was over. In 1965 my baseball card came out with no picture."

Bob Uecker (b. 1935)
American baseball player and sportscaster

"My wife and family are very pleased. They all forgot I had a good disposition."

Frank Broyles (b. 1924)
American university athletic director
(on announcing his retirement as head coach at the University of Arkansas)

"Work is the basis of living. I'll never retire. A man'll rust out quicker than he'll wear out."

Col. Harland Sanders (1890–1980)
founder, Kentucky Fried Chicken

"Retirement is the ugliest word in the language."

Ernest Hemingway (1899–1961)
American journalist and writer

"Probably the Beatles' white album."

Steve Largent (b. 1954)
American football player and former U.S. Congressman
(when asked which record the Seattle Seahawks All-Pro receiver would treasure most when he retired)

"Everybody wants to go to heaven, but nobody wants to die."

Joe Louis (1914–1981)
World heavyweight boxing champion, 1937–1949

"Most people my age are dead."

Casey Stengel (1891–1975)
American baseball manager

"A man is not old till regrets take the place of dreams."

John Barrymore (1882–1942)
American actor

"If you've never seen a real, fully developed look of disgust, just tell your son how you conducted yourself when you were a boy."

Frank McKinney "Kin" Hubbard (1868–1930)
American humorist

"May you get to heaven a half hour before the devil knows you're dead."

Irish proverb

Part 6

Keys to Success in Sports

Chapter 21

Team Performance

"There'll be two buses leaving the hotel for the ballpark tomorrow. The two o'clock bus will be for those of you who need a little extra work. The empty bus will be leaving at five o'clock."

Dave Bristol (b. 1933)
American baseball manager

"I'm a great believer in luck, and I find the harder I work the more I have of it."

Thomas Jefferson (1743–1826)
3rd president of the United States (1801–1809)

"I consider myself blessed. I consider you blessed. We've all been blessed with God-given talents. Mine just happens to be beating people up."

Sugar Ray Leonard (b. 1956)
World welterweight (1980–1982) and middleweight (1987) boxing champion

"It's just a job. Grass grows, birds fly, waves pound the sand. I beat people up."

Muhammad Ali (b. 1942)
World heavyweight boxing champion, 1964–1967, 1974–1978

"If it ain't broke, don't fix it."

Bert Lance (b. 1931)
American banker and advisor to President Jimmy Carter

"I don't believe the old statement, 'If it ain't broke, don't fix it.' If that's the case, then Cadillacs and Jaguars and Mercedes would never make a change. I've always looked for ways to make things better."

Vic Bubas (b. 1926)
American basketball coach and athletic conference commissioner

"The difficult we do at once; the impossible takes a bit longer."

Inscription on the memorial to the SeaBees
(U.S. Naval Construction Batallions)

"Don't tell me how hard you work. Tell me how much you get done."

James Ling (b. 1922)
American business executive

"You can learn more character on the two-yard line than you can anywhere in life."

Paul Dietzel (b. 1924)
American college football coach

"If you'd only told me you was gonna pitch a no-hitter, I'd a pitched me one, too."

Jay Hanna "Dizzy" Dean (1910–1974)
American professional baseball player
(after brother Paul pitched a no-hitter following Dizzy's three-hitter in a doubleheader)

"The man who makes no mistakes does not usually make anything."

William Connor Magee (1821–1891)
Bishop of Peterborough

"Experience is the name everyone gives to their mistakes."

Oscar Wilde (1854–1900)
Irish poet, playwright, and novelist

"We always admire the other fellow more after we have tried to do his job."

William Feather (1889–1981)
American author and publisher

"The great majority of men are bundles of beginnings."

Ralph Waldo Emerson (1803–1882)
American essayist and poet

"The quality of a person's life is in direct proportion to their commitment to excellence, regardless of their chosen field of endeavor."

Vince Lombardi (1913–1970)
American professional football coach

"It is a funny thing about life; if you refuse to accept anything but the best, you very often get it."

Somerset Maugham (1874–1965)
English novelist and dramatist

"Even if you're on the right track, you'll get run over if you just sit there."

Will Rogers (1879–1935)
American actor and humorist

"The horse weighs one thousand pounds and I weigh ninety-five. I guess I'd better get him to cooperate."

Steve Cauthen (b. 1960)
American jockey

Chapter 22

MONEY

"Why do you think I'm fighting? The glory? The agony of defeat? You show me a man says he ain't fighting for money, I'll show you a fool."

Larry Holmes (b. 1949)
World heavyweight boxing champion, 1978

"Money is the driving factor. It's not for the love of it. You never see pro football players put on their helmets and pads in the off-season and say, 'Hey, let's play a little for the love of it.' You see basketball players get together, but not football players."

Johnny Sample (b. 1937)
American professional football player

"A lot of it is the money, but I'd be playing if I was making $150,000."

Reggie Jackson (b. 1946)
American professional baseball player

"You know, I signed with the Milwaukee Braves for $3,000. That bothered my dad at the time, because he didn't have that kind of dough to pay out. But eventually he scraped it up."

Bob Uecker (b. 1935)
American baseball player and sportscaster

"Maybe it is all just a matter of growing up. Fans do tend to be children. They try to pretend that the athlete of their fancy is out there doing what he excels at for some greater good or glory than a buck. That naïve view is probably the nub of the problem, and the fault lies with the fan, not the athlete who always knew he was playing for the dollars and not much else."

Mark H. McCormack (1930–2003)
founder and former chairman,
IMG Sports Management

"Cadillacs are down at the end of the bat."

Ralph Kiner (b. 1922)
American professional baseball player
(on why he emphasized home runs rather than choking up when he batted)

"I don't like money actually, but it quiets my nerves."

Joe Louis (1914–1981)
World heavyweight boxing champion, 1937–49

"The only thing tainted about money is, it 'taint mine' or 'taint enough.'"

Anonymous

"Ballplayers and deer hunters are alike. They both want the big bucks."

Larry Doughty (b. 1940)
American baseball club executive

"He wants Texas back."

Tommy Lasorda (b. 1927)
American baseball manager
(on contract negotiations with Mexican-born pitcher Fernando Valenzuela)

"When coaches said, 'Jump,' players used to say, 'How high?' Now they say, 'Why? Is it in my contract?'"

Brian Billick (b. 1956)
head coach, Baltimore Ravens

"People think we make $3 million and $4 million a year. They don't realize that most of us only make $500,000."

Pete Incaviglia (b. 1964)
American professional baseball player

"When I was in college I used to dream of the day when I might be earning the salary I can't get by on now."

Louis E. Boone (b. 1941)
American educator and business writer

"Money, it turned out, was exactly like sex. You thought of nothing else if you didn't have it and thought of other things if you did."

James Baldwin (1924–1987)
American novelist and essayist

"Money bewitches people. They fret for it, and they sweat for it. They devise most ingenious ways to get it and most ingenious ways to get rid of it. Money is the only commodity that is good for nothing but to be gotten rid of. It will not feed you, clothe you, shelter you, or amuse you unless you spend it or invest it. It imparts value only in parting. People will do almost anything for money, and money will do almost anything for people. Money is a captivating, circulating, and masquerading puzzle."

Unknown

"Investing is like batting in baseball, except that you get as many pitches as you want and you never have to swing. Wait for the home run ball before investing."

Warren Buffett (b. 1930)
billionaire American investor and 25 percent owner of the Omaha Royals minor-league baseball club

"Money doesn't talk; it swears."

Bob Dylan (b. 1941)
American singer and songwriter

"It's like going into a nuclear war with bows and arrows."

Joe Kinnear (b. 1946)
Irish-born soccer team manager
(comparing resources and finances for major-market versus small-market sports teams)

"The bowling alley is the poor man's country club."

Sanford Hansell
American bowling center manager

"I used to think I was poor. Then they told me I wasn't poor, I was needy. They told me it was self-defeating to think of myself as needy. I was deprived. Then they told me underprivileged was overused. I was disadvantaged. I still don't have a dime. But I have a great vocabulary."

Jules Feiffer (b. 1929)
American cartoonist, novelist, playwright, and screenwriter

"The question isn't at what age I want to retire, it's at what income."

George Foreman (b. 1949)
World heavyweight boxing champion, 1973–1974

"If you want to know what God thinks of money, look at the people he gives it to."

Yiddish proverb

"Show me the money."

Cuba Gooding, Jr. (b. 1967)
American actor
(in Cameron Crowe's 1996 motion picture Jerry Maguire*)*

"We had so little to eat that when Mom would throw a bone to the dog, he'd have to call for a fair catch."

Lee Trevino (b. 1939)
American professional golfer

"If you think nobody cares if you're alive, try missing a couple of car payments."

Earl Wilson (1907–1987)
American newspaper columnist

"You don't see me at Vegas or at the races throwing my money around. I've got a government to support."

Bob Hope (1903–2003)
British-born actor and comedian

PERKS AND PAY

Even though the *average* salary in sports like major league baseball and the NBA long ago passed the $1 million mark, every once in a while, it's not the pay—but the perks—that separate deal makers from deal breakers. Here are a few examples.

Player	Perk
Kevin Brown	The Los Angeles Dodgers closed the deal with this star pitcher (since traded to the New York Yankees) by providing 12 private-jet trips a year for his family from Macon, Georgia to Los Angeles.
Kaz Matsui	To entice the all-star Japanese shortstop, the Mets agreed to pay up to $100,000 for two translators, one for him at the ballpark and another for his family.
Nomar Garciaparra	If traded, the Boston Red Sox would pay the difference if his home sold below its appraised value.
Greg Maddox	Today, every major leaguer is guaranteed his own private room on the road, but Maddox, Curt Schilling, and a few other baseball All-Stars get hotel suites.
Alex Rodriguez	Part of the deal that brought seven-time All-Star A-Rod from Texas to New York was the offer of a hotel suite on road trips, the right to link his Web site to the Yankees' site, and a guarantee that his deferred income could not be wiped out by a work stoppage.

But such special treatment is not limited to athletes. Singer Christina Aguilera's contract calls for her concert dressing rooms to be supplied with Flintstones vitamins and Boys II Men have standing requests for two dozen black towels.

Chapter

23

RECORDS, RESULTS, AND STATISTICS

"If winning isn't important, why do they keep score?"

Adolph Rupp (1901–1977)
American college basketball coach

"Baseball is the only field of endeavor where a man can succeed three times out of ten and be considered a good performer."

Ted Williams (1918–2002)
American professional baseball player

"Close doesn't count in baseball. Close only counts in horseshoes and grenades."

Frank Robinson (b. 1935)
American baseball player and manager
(first African American manager in the major leagues)

"Hit the ball over the fence and you can take your time going around the bases."

John W. Raper (1870–1950)
American author

"Expect the worst and your surprises will always be pleasant ones."

Louis E. Boone (b. 1941)
American educator and business writer

"Eighty percent of all surprises are unpleasant. This includes bills, estimates, unkept promises, firings, birthday parties, and pregnancies."

William A. Marsteller (b. 1914)
American advertising agency executive

"No one wants to quit when he's losing and no one wants to quit when he's winning."

Richard Petty (b. 1937)
American auto racing champion

"Statistics are to baseball what a flaky crust is to Mom's apple pie."

Harry Reasoner (1923–1991)
American television news reporter

"Learn to write. Never mind the damn statistics. If you like statistics, become a CPA."

Jim Murray (1919–2003)
American sports writer

"I didn't care about the statistics to anything else. I didn't and don't pay attention to statistics on the stock market, the weather, the crime rate, the gross [domestic] product, the circulation of magazines, the ebb and flow of literacy among football fans and how many people are going to starve to death before the year 2050 if I don't start adopting them for $3.69 a month. Just baseball. Now why is that? It is because baseball statistics, unlike the statistics in any other area, have acquired the powers of language."

Bill James
American writer and author, The Baseball Almanac

"He uses statistics as a drunken man uses lamp posts—for support rather than illumination."

Andrew Lang (1844–1912)
Scottish scholar and author

"If all the people who fell asleep watching golf on television were laid end to end, they would be a lot more comfortable."

David L. Kurtz (b. 1941)
American educator and business writer

"Just try explaining the value of statistical summaries to the widow of the man who drowned crossing a stream with an average depth of four feet."

Anonymous

"Hey, I have everything to be happy about, but I'm not. In the eyes of the media and my peers, I'm having a very good season, perhaps my best. I'm leading the league in scoring, but happiness in pro basketball is determined in the won-and-lost column, and we're not winning. Statistics are for losers."

"Pistol" Pete Maravich (1948–1988)
American basketball player

"They can make 250 bats from one good tree. How's that for a statistic, baseball fans?"

Andy Rooney (b. 1919)
American author and news commentator

"There are two kinds of statistics, the kind you look up and the kind you make up."

Rex Stout (1886–1975)
American mystery writer

"There are three kinds of lies: lies, damned lies, and statistics."

Benjamin Disraeli (1804–1881)
British prime minister

"The rule on staying alive as a forecaster is to give 'em a number or give 'em a date, but never give 'em both at once."

Jane Bryant Quinn (b. 1939)
American business writer

"A horse that can count to ten is a remarkable horse, not a remarkable mathematician."

Samuel Johnson (1709–1784)
English lexicographer and author

"Reporting facts is the refuge of those who have no imagination."

Luc de Clapiers
Marquis de Vauvenargues (1715–1747)
French soldier and moralist

"Baseball isn't statistics, it's Joe DiMaggio rounding second base."

Jimmy Breslin (b. 1930)
American sportswriter

"Torture the data long enough and they will confess to anything."

Anonymous

"We are drowning in information but starved for knowledge."

John Naisbitt (b. 1929)
American business writer and social researcher

"The public never forgives a guy who dents an idol, profanes an icon, or shows up Santa Claus. You can kill all the buffalo, wipe out the cavalry, rob all the banks, sell the State house, run rum, or join the Mafia—but don't mess around with America's sports idolatry. They don't forgive the guy who floored Dempsey, beat Willie Pep, ambushed Billy the Kid, hit more homers than Babe Ruth, shot more birdies than Hogan, or overtook Arnold Palmer."

Jim Murray (1919–2003)
American sports columnist

"Statistics are about as interesting as first-base coaches."

Jim Bouton (b. 1939)
American baseball player and author

Part 7

A Broader Perspective

Chapter 24

Ethics in Sports

"Sports do not build character. They reveal it."

Heywood Hale Broun (1888–1955)
American journalist

"Try to hate your opponent. Even if you are playing your grandmother, try to beat her fifty to nothing. If she already has three, try to beat her fifty to three."

Danny McGoorty (1903–1970)
English comic

"What are we out at the park for except to win? I'd trip my mother. I'll help her up, brush her off, tell her I'm sorry. But Mother don't make it to third."

Leo Durocher (1905–1991)
American baseball player and manager

"Grandmother was a pretty good hitter."

Early Wynn (1920–1999)
American professional baseball player
(when asked if he would really brush back his own grandmother)

"I'm not Mother Teresa."

Mike Tyson (b. 1956)
American boxer

"They shouldn't throw at me. I'm the father of five or six kids."

Tito Fuentes (b. 1944)
Cuban-born professional baseball player

"The time is always right to do what is right."

Martin Luther King, Jr. (1929–1968)
American clergyman and civil rights leader

"One man practicing sportsmanship is far better than 50 preaching it."

Knute Rockne (1888–1931)
Norwegian-born college football coach

"People should know what you stand for. They should also know what you won't stand for."

Anonymous

"Tarkanian has never been scrupulous about his players' academic credentials. I believe that now at Fresno State, he would sign Slobodan Milosevic if he needed a blood-thirsty pompadoured Balkan point guard."

Charles P. Pierce (b. 1953)
American journalist
(on former UNLV basketball coach Jerry Tarkanian)

"There's always room at the top—after the investigation."

Oliver Herford (1863–1935)
English writer and illustrator

"Take a look at them. All nice guys. They'll finish last. Nice guys finish last."

Leo Durocher (1905–1991)
American baseball manager
(observing the New York Giants in 1946)

"A good sport has to lose to prove it."

Anonymous

"It is hard to believe that a man is telling the truth when you know that you would lie if you were in his place."

H. L. Mencken (1880–1956)
American editor

"Two things are bad for the heart—running uphill and running down people."

Bernard Gimbel (1885–1966)
American merchant

"Nobody ever forgets where he buried a hatchet."

Frank McKinney "Kin" Hubbard (1868–1930)
American humorist

"Trust everybody, but cut the cards."

Finley Peter Dunne (1867–1936)
American humorist

"I'm honored that you invited me, especially when for $10,000 and a new convertible you could have had the top running-back prospect at SMU."

Tom Brokaw (b. 1940)
American television newscaster
(as master of ceremonies for a National Collegiate Athletic Association honors luncheon)

"You couldn't pay me to go to an SWC school."

Benny Perry (b. 1970)
heavily recruited Texas high school football player
(on his lack of interest in playing at a Southwest Conference university)

"They'll fire you for losing before they'll fire you for cheating."

Darryl Rogers (b. 1935)
American college football coach

"For when the One Great Scorer comes
To write against your name,
He marks—not that you won or lost—
But how you played the game."

Grantland Rice (1880–1954)
American sportswriter

"We demean the profession when we cheat. Coaching's not a job, it's a privilege."

Lee Corso (b. 1935)
American college football coach and sportscaster

"Well, this year I'm told the team did well because one pitcher had a fine curve ball. I understand that a curve ball is thrown with a deliberate attempt to deceive. Surely that is not an ability we should want to foster at Harvard."

Charles William Eliot (1834–1926)
President, Harvard University (1869–1909)
(explaining why he wanted to drop baseball as a college sport)

"Every man has his price."

Robert Walpole (1676–1745)
English statesman

"The pressures to win are getting unreal. Football and basketball are the income producers and, if you don't sell tickets, you're out of a job. So a coach who needs a player real bad will bend the rules a little to keep him eligible. Once you bend them a little, you bend them a little more."

Charlie McClendon (1923–2000)
American college football coach

"At this moment, America's greatest economic need is higher ethical standards—standards enforced by strict laws and upheld by responsible business leaders. There is no capitalism without conscience, there is no wealth without character."

George W. Bush (b. 1946)
43rd president of the United States (2001–)

"To imitate one's enemy is to dishonor."

Thomas Hobbes (1588–1679)
English philosopher

"Be good and you will be lonesome."

Mark Twain (1835–1910)
American author

"An injury is much sooner forgotten than an insult."

Philip Dormer Stanhope (1694–1773)
Earl of Chesterfield
English statesman and author

"All the things I really like to do are either immoral, illegal, or fattening."

Alexander Woollcott (1887–1943)
American writer

"Start with what is right rather than what is acceptable."

Peter Drucker (b. 1909)
American business philosopher and author

"We have the cleanest professional sport of all. In baseball, if a guy traps a ball, he doesn't call it on himself; he tries to fool the umpire. We police ourselves. I've seen people call two-stroke penalties on themselves when it meant a $150,000 tournament."

Bruce Crampton (b. 1935)
Australian-born professional golfer

"Golf is a game in which you yell Fore, shoot six, and write down five."

Paul Harvey (b. 1918)
American newscaster

"I used to play golf with a guy who cheated so badly that he once had a hole in one and wrote down zero on his scorecard."

Bob Brue
American professional golfer

Thou shalt not use profanity.
Thou shalt not covet thy neighbor's putter.
Thou shalt not steal thy neighbor's ball.
Thou shalt not bear false witness in the final tally.

Ground Rules for a Grand Rapids, Michigan,
Ministers' Golf Tournament

"Serious sport has nothing to do with fair play. It is bound up with hatred, jealousy, boastfulness, disregard of all rules, and sadistic pleasure in witnessing violence. In other words, it is war minus the shooting."

George Orwell (1903–1950)
English author

"Win any way you can as long as you can get away with it."

Leo Durocher (1905–1991)
American baseball manager

"Sportsmanship, next to the Church, is the greatest teacher of morals."

Herbert Hoover (1874–1964)
31st president of the United States (1929–1933)

"Fishermen don't lie. They just tell beautiful stories."

Syngman Rhee (1875–1965)
First president of the Republic of Korea

"Man is the only animal that blushes—or needs to."

Mark Twain (1835–1910)
American author

"When a man sells eleven ounces for twelve, he makes a compact with the devil, and sells himself for the value of an ounce."

Henry Ward Beecher (1813–1887)
American clergyman and writer

"Live in such a way that you would not be ashamed to sell your parrot to the town gossip."

Will Rogers (1879–1935)
American actor and humorist

TEN COMMANDMENTS OF SPORT

1. Thou shalt not quit.
2. Thou shalt not alibi.
3. Thou shalt not gloat over winning.
4. Thou shalt not sulk over losing.
5. Thou shalt not take unfair advantage.
6. Thou shalt not ask odds thou art unwilling to give.
7. Thou shalt always be willing to give thine opponent the benefit of the doubt.
8. Thou shalt not underestimate an opponent or overestimate thyself.
9. Remember that the game is the thing and he who thinks otherwise is not a true sportsman.
10. Honor the game thou playest, for he who plays the game straight and hard wins even when he loses.

Chapter 25

Creating a Color-blind Sports World

"I have always said it's more important who's going to be the first black sports editor of the *New York Times* than the first black baseball manager."

Bill Russell (b. 1934)
American professional basketball player and coach

"Sport is the only place we have left where we can start even."

Paul W. "Bear" Bryant (1913–1983)
American college football coach

"In the field of sports you are more or less accepted for what you do rather than what you are."

Althea Gibson (1927–2003)
American professional tennis player
(In 1957, the first African American—male or female— to win at Wimbledon)

"You know it's going to be hell when the best rapper out there is a white guy and the best golfer is a black guy."

Charles Barkley (b. 1963)
American professional basketball player

"Very few blacks will take up golf until the requirement for plaid pants is dropped."

Franklin Ajaye (b. 1949)
American actor

"Boxing is the one opportunity for the low man on the ethnic totem pole. It is a short cut to money, prestige, status, power."

Cus D'Amato (1907–1985)
American boxing manager

"We will have differences. Men of different ancestries, men of different tongues, men of different colors, men of different environments, men of different geographies do not see everything alike. Even in our own country we do not see everything alike. If we did, we would all want the same wife—and that would be a problem, wouldn't it?"

Lyndon B. Johnson (1908–1973)
36th president of the United States (1963–1969)

"I'm not concerned with your liking or disliking me . . . . All I ask is that you respect me as a human being."

Jackie Robinson (1919–1972)
American professional baseball player

"Robinson could hit and bunt and steal and run. He had intimidating skills, and he burned with a dark fire. He wanted passionately to win . . . . He bore the burden of a pioneer and the weight made him more strong. If one can be certain of anything in baseball, it is that we shall not look upon his like again."

Roger Kahn (b. 1927)
American author and sportswriter

"All the courage and competitiveness of Jackie Robinson affects me to this day. If I patterned my life after anyone it was him. Not because he was the first black baseball player in the majors but because he was a hero."

Kareem Abdul-Jabbar (b. 1947)
American professional basketball player

"Every time I look at my pocketbook, I see Jackie Robinson."

Willie Mays (b. 1931)
American professional baseball player

"The only change is that baseball has turned Paige from a second-class citizen into a second-class immortal."

Leroy Robert "Satchel" Paige (1904–1982)
American professional baseball player (on being included in a wing for Negro Baseball League stars in the Baseball Hall of Fame)

"He's a credit to his race—the human race."

Jimmy Cannon (1909–1973)
American sportswriter (on world heavyweight boxing champion Joe Louis)

"Prejudice is the child of ignorance."

William Hazlitt (1778–1830)
English critic and author

"America is not like a blanket—one piece of unbroken cloth, the same color, the same texture, the same size. America is more like a quilt—many pieces, many colors, many sizes, all woven and held together by a common thread."

Jesse Jackson (b. 1941)
American civil rights leader

"It doesn't matter if a cat is black or white, so long as it catches mice."

Deng Xiaoping (1904–1997)
Chinese premier (1979–1989)

"Prejudice saves a lot of time, because you can form an opinion without the facts."

Anonymous

"I strongly believe the black culture expends too much time, energy, and effort raising, praising, and teasing our black children about the dubious glories of professional sport. Your son has less than one chance in one thousand of becoming a pro. Would you bet your son's future on something with odds 999 to 1 against you? I wouldn't."

Arthur Ashe (1943–1993)
American professional tennis player

"Keep away from people who try to belittle your ambitions. Small people always do that, but the really great make you feel that you, too, can become great."

Mark Twain (1835–1910)
American author

"You can't play on a team with African-Americans for very long and fail to recognize the stupidity of our national obsession with race. The right path is really very simple. Give respect to teammates of a different race, treat them fairly, disagree with them honestly, enjoy their friendship, explore your common humanity, share your thoughts about one another candidly, work together for a common goal, help one another achieve it. No ridiculous fears. No debilitating anger."

Bill Bradley (b. 1943)
American professional basketball player
and U.S. Senator

"No one is any better than you, but you are no better than anyone else until you do something to prove it."

Donald Laird (1897–1967)
American psychologist

"No one can make you feel inferior without your consent."

Eleanor Roosevelt (1884–1962)
American humanitarian and writer

"It's always worthwhile to make others aware of their worth."

Malcolm Forbes (1919–1990)
American publisher

"A minority group has 'arrived' only when it has the right to produce some fools and scoundrels without the entire group paying for it."

Carl T. Rowan (b. 1925)
American columnist and diplomat

"He who will not reason is a bigot; he who cannot is a fool; and he who dares not is a slave."

Sir William Drummond (1854–1907)
Canadian poet

"The worst prejudice in sports isn't skin color; it's size."

Calvin Murphy (b. 1948)
5'9" American professional basketball player

"If you're small, you better be a winner."

Billie Jean King (b. 1943)
American professional tennis player

"Nobody roots for Goliath."

Wilt Chamberlain (1936–1999)
7'1" American professional basketball player

"Baseball is the only game left for people. To play basketball now, you have to be 7 ft. 6 in. To play football you have to be the same width."

Bill Veeck (1914–1986)
American baseball team owner

"When a jockey retires, he becomes just another little man."

Eddie Arcaro (1916–97)
American jockey

Bibliography

Armstrong, Lance, *Every Second Counts.* New York: Broadway Books, 2003.

Augustine, Norman R., *Augustine's Laws.* New York: Viking, 1986.

Barnett, Alex, *The Quotable American.* Guilford CT: The Lyons Press, 2002.

Beilenson, Peter, *Grand Slams and Fumbles: Sports Quotes.* White Plains, N.Y.: Peter Pauper Press, 1989.

Bishop, Morin, *They Said It.* New York: Oxmoor House, 1990.

Boller, Paul F., Jr., and John George, *They Never Said It.* New York: Oxford University Press, 1989.

Boone, Louis E., *Quotable Business,* Second Edition. New York: Random House, 1999.

Brunt, Stephen, *Facing Ali.* Guilford, CT: The Lyons Press, 2003.

Carruth, Gorton, and Eugene Ehrlich, *The Harper Book of American Quotations.* New York: Harper & Row, 1988.

_____, and Pat Sullivan, *Inside Golf: Quotations on the Royal and Ancient Game.* New York: Atheneum, 1985.

Crainer, Stuart, *The Ultimate Book of Business Quotations.* New York: AMACON, 1998.

Dickson, Paul, *Baseball's Greatest Quotations.* New York: Harper Perennial, 1992.

Fitzhenry, Robert I., *Barnes & Noble Book of Quotations.* New York: Barnes & Noble, 1987.

Frank, Leonard Roy, *Quotationary.* New York: Random House, 2001.

Freeman, Mike, *Bloody Sunday: Inside the Dazzling, Rough-and-Tumble World of the NFL.* New York: William Morrow, 2003.

Garagiola, Joe, *It's Anybody's Ballgame.* Chicago: Contemporary Books, 1988.

Graham, Stedman, Lisa Delpy Neirotti, and Joe Jeff Goldblatt, *The Ultimate Guide to Sports Marketing.* New York: McGraw-Hill, 2001.

Griffith, Joe, *Speaker's Library of Business Stories, Anecdotes and Humor.* Englewood Cliffs, NJ: Prentice-Hall, 1990.

Harris, Nick, *I Wish I'd Said That!* Secaucus, NJ: Castle, 1987.

Henry, Lewis C., *Best Quotations for All Occasions.* New York: Fawcett Premier, 1989.

Hoffman, Dale and Martin J. Greenberg, *Sportsbiz.* Champaign, IL: Leisure Press, 1989.

Jarman, Colin M., *The Nasty Quote Book.* New York: Gramercy Books, 2001.

Kent, Robert W., *Money Talks.* New York: Pocket Books, 1985.

Klatell, David A. and Norman Marcus, *Sports For Sale: Television, Money, and the Fans*. New York: Oxford University Press, 1988.
Knowles, Elizabeth, *The Oxford Dictionary of Twentieth Century Quotations.* New York: Oxford University Press, 1998.
Lewis, Michael, *Moneyball*. New York: Norton, 2003.
Liddle, Barry, *Dictionary of Sports Quotations*. London: Routledge & Kegan Paul, 1987.
Maggio, Rosalie, *The New Beacon Book of Quotations by Women*. Boston: Beacon Press, 1996.
Maikovich, Andrew J., *Sports Quotations*. Jefferson, NC: Houghton Mifflin, 1988.
Mays, Willie, *Say Hey: The Autobiography of Willie Mays*. New York: Simon & Schuster, 1988.
Metcalf, Fred, *The Penguin Dictionary of Modern Humorous Quotations.* London: Penguin Books, 1987.
Miller, James Edward, *The Baseball Business*. Chapel Hill: University of North Carolina Press, 1990.
Moore, Joe, *Have You Ever Noticed?* New York: Pocket Books, 1988.
Mullin, Bernard J., Stephen Hardy, and William A. Sutton, *Sport Marketing*. Champaign, IL: Human Kinetics, 2000.
Nack, William, *My Turf*. Cambridge, MA: Capo Press, 2003.
Partnow, Elaine, *The New Quotable Woman*. New York: Facts on File, 1992.
Platt, Suzy, *Respectfully Quoted*. Washington: Library of Congress, 1989.
Plimpton, George, *Plimpton on Sports*. Guilford CT: The Lyons Press, 2003.
Porter, David L., *Biographical Dictionary of American Sports: Baseball*. New York: Greenwood Press, 1987.
______, *Biographical Dictionary of American Sports: Football.* New York: Greenwood Press, 1987.
Queenan, Joe, *True Believers: The Tragic Inner Life of Sports Fans.* New York: Henry Holt, 2003.
Rawson, Hugh, and Margaret Miner, *The New International Dictionary of Quotations.* New York: NAL Books, 1986.
Reilly, Rick, *Who's Your Caddy?* New York: Doubleday, 2003.
Rotella, Carlo, *Cut Time*. Boston: Houghton Mifflin, 2003.
Scully, Gerald W., *The Business of Major League Baseball*. Chicago: University of Chicago Press, 1989.
Shafritz, Jay M., *Words on War: Military Quotations From Ancient Times to the Present.* Upper Saddle River, NJ: Prentice-Hall, 1990.
Shank, Matthew D., *Sports Marketing.* Upper Saddle River NJ: Prentice-Hall, 2002.
Shipps, Anthony W., *The Quote Sleuth: A Manual for the Tracer of Lost Quotations.* Urbana: University of Illinois Press, 1990.

Simpson, James B., *Simpson's Contemporary Quotations*. Boston: Houghton Mifflin, 1988.
Swainson, Bill, *Encarta Book of Quotations*. New York: St. Martin's Press, 2000.
Tomlinson, Gerald, *Speaker's Treasury of Sports Anecdotes, Stories, and Humor*. Englewood Cliffs, NJ: Prentice Hall, 1990.
Tripp, Rhoda Thomas, *The International Thesaurus of Quotations*. New York: Harper & Row, 1987.
Tuleja, Tad, *Quirky Quotations*. New York: Galahad Books, 2000.
Van Natta, Jr., Don, *First Off the Tee*. Cambridge, MA: Perseus Publishing, 2003.
White, Rolf B., *The Last Word on Management*. New York: Lyle Stuart, 1987.
Winkokur, Jon, *The Portable Curmudgeon*. New York: NAL Books, 1987.
_____, *A Curmudgeon's Garden of Love*. New York: NAL Books, 1989.
_____, *Friendly Advice*. New York: Dutton, 1990.

NAME INDEX

Subject Index